THE INTERSECTIONAL
ENVIRONMENTALIST

THE INTERSECTIONAL ENVIRONMENTALIST

How to Dismantle Systems of Oppression to Protect People + Planet

LEAH THOMAS

Voracious
Little, Brown and Company
NEW YORK BOSTON LONDON

Voracious / Little, Brown and Company
Hachette Book Group
1290 Avenue of the Americas, New York, NY 10104
littlebrown.com

First Edition: March 2022

Voracious is an imprint of Little, Brown and Company, a division
of Hachette Book Group, Inc. The Voracious name and logo are
trademarks of Hachette Book Group, Inc.

The publisher is not responsible for websites (or their content)
that are not owned by the publisher.

The Hachette Speakers Bureau provides a wide range
of authors for speaking events. To find out more, go to
hachettespeakersbureau.com or call (866) 376-6591.

ISBN 9780316279291
LCCN 2021943101

10 9 8 7 6 5 4 3 2

MOHN

Printed in Germany

To Camara, because every younger sister
knows their older sister is their very first
and forever best friend

CONTENTS

FOREWORD

Gloria Walton, president and CEO
of The Solutions Project

MY GRANDMOTHER, a farmer and descendent of people enslaved in the United States, was one of my greatest teachers, instilling in me foundational values of dignity, community, and love. I remember walking with her as a small child and her saying, with the sweetest Southern charm, "Walk in front of me, honey. Put your head up! Roll those shoulders back, swing those arms, smile, and walk with purpose, ba-by!" And I did!

She, alongside my mother and the matriarchs in our neighborhood, taught me that dignity comes from within—from the love I have for myself and my community. I was born into poverty, but I was raised by proud, resourceful Black women who took care of themselves, their people, and the land. I remember vividly how concepts like conservation and sustainable living were not theoretical to us, nor were they burdens to our way of life. They were how we got by, how we flowed in relationship to one another and our environment. We practiced the models that were passed down from generations before us, and we integrated our own experiences into lessons for the future.

My mother and grandmother made sure we didn't waste electricity or water. We reused grocery bags and canning jars, and we recycled hand-me-down clothing among our cousins. We carpooled with our neighbors to save gas and carefully stewarded what we had. We shared eggs and milk with neighbors, and we composted leftover food. We did this because we cared for one another and cared for the places we called home. I learned that caring is a practice that is good for people and good for the earth.

These grassroots values were specific results of our Black, mostly feminine, and poor lives, which of course also included immense pain and hardship as we were on the other end of every stick wielded by those in power and upheld by race, gender, and class.

I was reminded of this time and these intersections in my life when I read Leah Thomas's childhood stories of waste-free living out of necessity, when I read about her own relationships and joys living among three generations of Black women. I feel some of my experience and analysis reflected in short form on her Instagram feed and smile with recognition. Our paths first crossed when I was CEO of a grassroots climate justice organization in South Central Los Angeles and Leah was an intern at Patagonia. I am grateful that Leah helped elevate the term and meaning of "intersectional environmentalism," inviting all of you, dear readers, into its life-affirming vision and values during a global pandemic, an escalating climate crisis, and popular uprisings for racial justice.

Intersectionality is one of those breakthrough academic concepts—this one coined by the inimitable Kimberlé Crenshaw—that, for millions of people, including Black women like her, and like me and Leah, is simply how we live. Just as Kimberlé Crenshaw's own lived experience gave rise to this foundational framework of critical race theory, her story and scholarship have offered the world a glimpse into our daily reality. Seeing how we, as Black women, can transmute terror and trauma into a vision for something beautiful, collective, and strong is what makes intersectionality so critical to solving the global climate crisis. It is also what makes critical race theory so scary to those clinging on to treacherous power. Because if *we* can create the future we want despite the realities of not only racism, but also sexism, poverty, and other oppressive systems, imagine what all of us can do and be when those systems crumble and we are all free. As Leah says, the future is intersectional—just as the past and present are too.

The era of a single-savior, top-down, and siloed approach to change is over. The old way of thinking about environmentalism as a single, distinct issue is long gone, because people are seeing that the solutions to our problems come from within ourselves, and from within our communities. People are empowered and coming together to create the change they want to see, the future they want that reflects their values and visions. And our intersectional lives are at the center of it.

As Leah lays out in the book, it is up to us to change the status quo, because many gatekeepers in the climate movement are still catching up and most of their ideas continue to benefit the few. Intersectional-focused organizations working for climate equity and justice still receive less than 5 percent—by the most generous accounting—of the total $2.4 billion granted annually for the environment. Within *that*, an even smaller fraction goes to nonprofits led by Black people, Indigenous people, immigrants, and other people of color. Women of color receive just 0.6 percent of total philanthropic *benefit* in the United States across all issue areas, despite being the backbones of most communities.

This is why, as Leah explains in this book, the fundamental truth is that we cannot save the planet without uplifting the voices of those most marginalized. These solutions are already being born from organizers in communities of color on the front lines of the climate crisis, many of whom have lived experiences that give meaning to intersectional environmentalism, even if they've never called it that.

As CEO of The Solutions Project, I've had the privilege of working with many of these organizers as they address the issues facing their communities. Take Louisiana's "cancer alley," where over two hundred petrochemical plants line eighty miles of the Mississippi River. The EPA says the cancer risk for the area's majority Black population is up to fifty times the national average. When the local government quickly granted permits for a new $1.25 billion plastics plant that would further poison the area with toxic chemicals, former teacher Sharon Lavigne and the community-based organization she leads, RISE St. James, organized, mobilized, and ultimately stopped the plant from being built. They gained recognition from the United Nations, Sharon was honored with the prestigious Goldman Environmental Prize, and her story was covered in *People* magazine.

Other everyday heroes come from the Four Corners region of the western United States, where fifteen thousand Hopi and Navajo families live in homes without electricity. This is despite decades of outsiders benefiting from coal, uranium, oil, and gas extracted from reservation land. Two Navajo women—organizer Wahleah Johns and engineer Suzanne Singer, PhD—started Native Renewables to design and deploy affordable solar photovoltaic arrays and storage systems that can, for the first time, bring electricity to far-flung off-the-grid homes on the reservation. Native Renewables also trains Indigenous people for clean-energy jobs. Now Johns is senior advisor for the Department of Energy's Office of Indian Energy Policy and Programs, seeking to apply her experience to helping the more than five hundred other Indigenous nations within the borders of the United States.

The success of these women, alongside their communities, shows that a people-powered movement works—and benefits everyone. We need big, sustainable solutions that benefit the many, not just the few. And all of us can be a part of it. We all live at various inter-sections, and when we can see that, the invitations to participate are everywhere.

We can also hold on to the grassroots values that will create a regenerative, healthy, and equitable planet. These values connect us to our family, to our communities, and ultimately to one another. It is audacious—and requires tenacity—to have a vision for a world one cannot materially see. It takes courage to challenge old ways and cre-ate new ones. And it requires love. After all, love is the source of this transformational power. Love for ourselves, our people, and the land. My grandmother, my mother, and the grassroots leaders I've worked with have shown me that courage, dignity, and love are abundant no matter the circumstance.

Leah Thomas's vision and this book are powerful testaments to this truth, and beautiful invitations for all of us to be a part of the future we want. Every day, more and more people are responding to a society mired in racism, sexism, injustice, and inequity by showing the rest of the world how justice is done. And this is just the beginning.

I look forward to seeing *your* contribution.

THE INTERSECTIONAL
ENVIRONMENTALIST

INTRODUCTION

WE CAN'T save the planet without uplifting the voices of its people, especially those most often unheard. We should care about the protection of people as much as we care about the protection of our planet—to me, these fights are the same. As a society, we often forget that humans are a part of our global ecosystem and that we don't exist separately from nature; we coexist with it each and every day.

Unfortunately, as with other animals, some humans are endangered and facing a multitude of social and environmental injustices that impact their ability to not only survive but also thrive in liberation and joy. Why, then, are conservation efforts not extended to the protection of endangered humans and their human rights? This is a question I've struggled with as a Black environmentalist for years, because in my environmental practice, caring for the earth means caring for its people.

The earth shouldn't be taken for granted, nor should its people, and the drivers of this exploitation—greed, racism, capitalism, and other systems of oppression—should be rejected and dismantled. If we combine social justice efforts with environmental awareness efforts, we will harness enough power, representation, and momentum to have a shot at protecting our planet and creating equity at the same time.

When I studied environmental science and policy as an undergrad at a predominantly white institution, social issues were perpetually separated from environmentalism, sustainability, and conservation. Learning about environmental justice wasn't mandatory in my liberal arts education, nor did I ever have a professor who looked like me—a stark contrast to the equity- and liberation-centered environment intertwined in curriculums at many historically Black colleges and universities. As a Black student in STEM, I had to search beyond the classroom to learn about the contributions of people of color to sustainability, and I had to conduct independent research projects to explore the social determinants that caused environmental injustice along racial, class, and gender lines.

This became increasingly frustrating over time, because I knew that my identity informed the way I cared for the world, from the cultural traditions passed down by my family to the realities of living in a country built from systemic oppression. I knew, even if it wasn't acknowledged, that the overwhelmingly white and middle-class identities of my peers, professors, and textbook authors influenced both what they prioritized as the most "urgent" issues facing the planet and what solutions they proposed. These often excluded the advocacy of racial equality.

The lack of representation of Black, Brown, Indigenous, Asian, low-income, LGBTQ+, disabled, and other marginalized voices has led to an ineffective form of mainstream environmentalism that doesn't truly stand for the liberation of all people and the planet. If it did, environmental injustice outcomes wouldn't be so closely linked to different identity aspects—as we'll explore in this book. From the data, it's evident that social justice and environmentalism are deeply intertwined and that addressing this interconnection is crucial for attaining justice for both people and planet.

Social injustice and environmental injustice are fueled by the same flame: the undervaluing, commodification, and exploitation of all forms of life and natural resources, from the smallest blade of grass to those living in poverty and oppressed people worldwide. It's a point that many ecofeminists, environmental justice scholars and leaders, Indigenous rights and land sovereignty advocates, and climate politicians have argued for decades, but it hasn't been embedded deeply enough in modern environmental education.

After years of dreaming about becoming an environmentalist, I was heartbroken to discover in my studies how the global environmental community has historically disregarded and silenced people of color, a breach that carries on today. In the largest environmental movements in the U.S. and worldwide, issues of race have been met with hostility, downplayed, questioned, and placed on the back burner. Because environmental justice activists, who are primarily Black, Latinx, Indigenous, and people of color, haven't been given the support from the global environmental community that they deserve, we are still fighting for climate justice all these years later.

I have stood alongside my white environmentalist peers at climate protests and worked alongside them in my environmental studies and while working in corporate sustainability and beyond, yet I felt abandoned by the environmental community during acts of unjustifiable violence against people of color. Even though I've witnessed the horrifying reality of Black people being mistreated during protests, I still showed up for climate protests. Even when the leadership of these climate protests wasn't diverse or when environmental justice wasn't on the agenda, I lent myself to the cause. I passionately adhered to the status quo of environmentalism because I felt like I was doing my duty for the planet and hoped that if I proved myself to be a loyal follower, then maybe advocacy of my people would be brought to the table.

But patience begins to run out and internal fires begin to burn when you're silencing parts of yourself. Did the environmental leaders I followed understand the gravity of risk associated with Black citizens across the world who faced violence for public demonstration? Did they understand the fear that I felt at every protest I've attended since watching nonviolent protesters in Ferguson be beaten, maced, and terrorized and Black reporters harassed and jailed? This disconnect was isolating. I watched predominantly white environmental protesters chain themselves to buildings, illegally deface property, trespass, and flaunt their arrests on camera during their protests, and I started to wonder: how? When nonviolent protesters or innocent Black, Indigenous, Latinx, and Asian citizens are met with injustice for smaller infractions, such as existing, I had to ask: how privileged must one be to so boldly participate in theatrical protests?

I had a rude awakening during the summer of 2014. While on break from college in my hometown of Florissant, Missouri, I received a call from a childhood friend asking if I'd known Michael Brown. I searched for his name in my memories and didn't find it, but little did I know that I, and the world, would soon know it forever. She broke the news to me that an unarmed Black teenager had been murdered by a police officer in an act of excessive violence (over six shots were fired from a significant distance); Brown's body lay in the street for hours as the surrounding community tried to piece together what had happened without communication from authorities or news outlets. Tension boiled and uprisings soon followed; my sister and parents headed to vigils and protests. But I had to leave to go back to Southern California to start work toward my newly declared major in environmental science.

While I was in my introductory environmental classes, I couldn't focus. How could I think about the Clean Air Act when my community was burning with smoke and tear gas? Spending time in nature during the aftermath of Ferguson helped me process the trauma that was unfolding back home, but I felt a deep sense of guilt at the same time and a kind of survivor's remorse. While I could easily go to the beach or hike in sunny California after my classes, my family and friends at home were dodging tear gas during protests to fight for my civil rights. Why was I entitled to clean air, water, and an abundance of nature in this privileged and wealthy Orange County community when places, like Ferguson, around the country were not? This kind of disparity persists not only in times of unrest but in general, due to lack of environmental protections in communities of color, which inevitably results in higher instances of environmental hazards.

As I started exploring the data behind environmental injustice, I came to see that this perception of inequality was far from just a hunch. The more I turned the pages of textbooks and peer-reviewed articles on environmental injustice, the more I saw time and time again that people of color in the U.S. and around the world are bearing the brunt of the climate crisis and environmental injustice. Alarm bells were going off in my head, and yet my ideas were met with confusion or dismissal in my classes and in primarily white environmental spaces, both corporate and political. I witnessed cognitive dissonance and gaslighting and was made to feel like my acknowledgment of racial injustice or sexism was disruptive—that my very presence was disruptive, no matter how meek I was or how much I tried to shrink myself.

After the trauma of Ferguson, I was acutely attuned to subsequent events like the police-related murders of Tamir Rice, Sandra Bland, and Breonna Taylor. Each headline filled me with heartbreak and left me wondering "When will it stop?" I hit my breaking point when I heard the last words of a Black father, George Floyd, streaming across social media. "I can't breathe," he repeated while a police officer kneeled on his neck as he lay handcuffed on the ground. He died by asphyxiation, and his death was later ruled a homicide.

His final words matched those of Eric Garner, another Black father, who was murdered by excessive force by New York City police after being detained in a chokehold for selling untaxed cigarettes in 2014. I hit my breaking point, as many environmentalists did during the Black Lives Matter movement uprisings of 2020. I felt alone and unheard, without much acknowledgment from the wider environmental community.

I couldn't do it anymore; I needed to immediately depart environmental spaces that ignored the urgent need for social justice reform. Advocating for the human rights of my people, and so many other oppressed identities worldwide, simply cannot be optional. I didn't want to be an "environmentalist" if that meant I had to choose between racial progress and environmental progress. Leaning into the theories of Black feminism and intersectional feminism, I found a home in what I call intersectional environmentalism. It would prioritize the concerns of my people and all marginalized people in addition to the protection of the planet.

So I thought about how a safer type of environmental practice could be defined, and I wrote it out a week after the murder of George Floyd on May 25, 2020. Stuck inside during the early stages of the COVID-19 pandemic, I took my protest art to the digital realm and created a text-based graphic that read "Environmentalists for Black Lives Matter" over and over in repeating rows. I created another slide with my definition of intersectional environmentalism, followed by a pledge with action steps for dismantling systems of oppression in the environmental movement, as well as steps for showing how to be an ally. I posted these materials online for anyone who wanted to join me. I was furloughed from my job and felt I had nothing to lose; I never could have imagined what followed.

Hundreds of thousands of people followed me on social media, reached out, and shared the pledge and graphic. Intersectional environmentalism grew on Google's search engines almost overnight, and some of the world's top environmental organizations—Greenpeace, Extinction Rebellion, NRDC, Fridays for Future, the Sierra Club, Patagonia, and beyond—shared the viral graphic and advocated for an intersectional approach to environmentalism. I suddenly didn't feel so alone anymore as I saw how millions of people around the world were ready to learn more about intersectional environmentalism and the legacy of climate justice and reshape the narrative of environmentalism to be more inclusive.

As I dove deeper into the history of environmental justice, I also realized that I was never alone in the first place—nor are other environmentalists of color. As cofounder of the Intersectional Environmentalist council Diandra Marizet says, "Our ancestors are activists," and even though we sometimes feel underrepresented or alone, our histories and cultures flow through the foundations of what is now considered "sustainability" and have done so since long before that phrasing even existed.

To ensure our organization would be rooted in community, we put together a collective of environmentalists for the first Intersectional Environmentalist council with varying perspectives and backgrounds, and we learned so much along the way. The first council included:

* **LEAH THOMAS,** founder of Intersectional Environmentalist
* **DIANDRA MARIZET,** cofounder of Intersectional Environmentalist
* **SABS KATZ,** cofounder of Intersectional Environmentalist
* **PHIL AIKEN,** cofounder of Intersectional Environmentalist
* **TERESA BAKER,** founder of the Outdoor CEO Diversity Pledge and founder of the In Solidarity Project

9

* **JOSÉ GONZÁLEZ,** founder and director emeritus of Latino Outdoors
* **PINAR SINOPOULOS-LLOYD,** cofounder of Queer Nature
* **ADITI MAYER,** labor rights activist, photojournalist, and sustainable fashion blogger
* **MARIE BEECHAM,** climate and racial justice advocate
* **SOPHIA LI,** multimedia journalist and film director
* **WYN WILEY / PATTIE GONIA,** drag queen and intersectional environmentalist / photographer, creative director, and outdoorist
* **RON GRISWELL,** founder and executive director of HBCUs Outside
* **MIKAELA LOACH,** climate justice activist and cohost of the *Yikes* podcast
* **ISAIAS HERNANDEZ,** creator of Queer Brown Vegan
* **KEVIN J. PATEL,** founder and executive director of OneUpAction
* **ABIGAIL ABHAER ADEKUNBI THOMAS,** environmentalist and environmental advocate
* **ANUSHKA BHASKAR,** founder of Avritah and the HEAL Program
* **JORDAN MARIE DANIEL,** founder of Rising Hearts
* **KAMILAH JOURNÉT,** marketing strategist, writer, and distance runner
* **ANDREA PEREZ,** Indigenous environmental justice advocate and geospatial analyst
* **JORDAN CHATMAN,** brand strategist and multimedia environmentalist
* **KRISTY DRUTMAN,** digital strategist and host of *Brown Girl Green*
* **SAGE LENIER,** environmental educator

Our next step was to build a database and accessible media and resource hub with action steps, resources, and information to dismantle systems of oppression in the environmental movement and explore the links between climate and social justice from a variety of perspectives. Education is often the first step in taking action, and when educational resources tell a more diverse and holistic story of environmentalism, people feel empowered and are more prone to take informed and intentional action.

This sudden grassroots momentum taught me that we are all participants in an online ecosystem, and we have the potential to make a greener, safer, and more equitable future for everyone, through our social media clicks and even more so in our real lives. If we want to see more inclusive movements, we can unite to create them and forge a new future for environmentalism together.

Environmental movements in the Global North—the wealthiest industrialized countries, many of which have benefited from colonization and are primarily concentrated in the northern part of the world—have failed to be truly inclusive for decades, from the advent of the Earth Day movement to the present. The largest environmental organizations in the world are grappling with internal and external legacies of racism, even within environmental policies and government agencies. Black, Brown, Indigenous, and impoverished people, and many communities in the Global South—countries that are newly becoming, or moving toward becoming, industrialized and often have a history of colonialism—are facing environmental injustices at alarming rates. Those least responsible for the climate crisis are bearing the brunt of it.

I can no longer take part in a type of environmentalism that would allow these oversights and injustices to continue, and I invite you to join me. Without swift action and a deeper look at the ways social injustice flows through environmental movements and policies, the advocacy of my people will continue to be brushed aside. It is time to

CHAPTER 1

Intersectional Theory, Feminism +
Intersectional Environmentalism

AS WE dive into what intersectionality means, it's important to note that this theory stems from the thoughts, experiences, and emotional labor of Black women. It may evolve and take shape in different ways past its original intent, as with environmentalism, but this theory, defined by Kimberlé Williams Crenshaw, is rooted in the duality of her experience as both Black and a woman. Any advancement or more broad adoption of intersectional theory should start with the fact that it was bred from the Black experience and was developed as a tool to help Black women feel seen, heard, and validated in their everyday lives. This theory reflects their experiences as they grappled with those two marginalized identities and faced double, interlocking oppressions and judgment. As Malcolm X said in a 1962 speech,

The most disrespected person in America is the Black woman.
The most unprotected person in America is the Black woman.
The most neglected person in America is the Black woman.[1]

Black women deserve both protection and appreciation. So as we continue to explore and dive deeper into intersectionality and intersectional environmentalism in this chapter, hold space for Black women. Protect and respect their theories and their profound resiliency; know that even in their struggle, Black women have given their knowledge to us to grow and advance society. It is an immense privilege to create space for and hold a piece of their magic and legacies every time the word "intersectionality" is said or written down—so don't use it lightly and please don't dilute its origins.

DIVISION IN THE FEMINIST MOVEMENT

THIS SECTION will refer to the women's rights movement, also called the feminist movement and the women's liberation movement, in the United States. First wave feminist movements of the nineteenth and early twentieth centuries, which predate the women's rights movement, largely focused on the advocacy of legal rights for women (like the ability to vote, receive an education, and secure employment).[2] Unfortunately, a recurrence through the different feminist movements in the United States is the lack of consideration for, and even hostile rejection of, racial equality within women's rights efforts.

The women's rights movement in the 1960s and '70s, considered second wave feminism, broadened the idea of what equality could look like for women and included sexual liberation, workplace safety, reproductive rights, the deconstruction of gender roles, and more.[3] But even with this broader feminism, the advocacy for women of color was not a focal point of the mainstream movement at large— nor did the movement give special consideration to queer and trans women. The dire need for safe spaces for women who weren't repre- sented in the mainstream movement led to an emerging Black fem- inist movement that advocated for both race and women's equality during the height of the civil rights and women's rights movements. This is where the seeds of intersectional theory were planted—which was later defined in 1989 by Kimberlé Williams Crenshaw.

What was the key goal of the second wave feminist women's rights movement? I think a fair answer would be the equality of women in all sectors of life. This is an admirable goal, but if those who are setting these goals aren't representative of all women, all women won't be equally protected as a result. Even if everyone is united by the common thread of being women, there is a danger when what's being considered a universal women's experience is only reflective of those who are privileged in other crucially defining areas in society, like race, class, and sexuality.

The understanding of a "universal women's experience" within the mainstream women's rights movement did not include strong consideration for the role that race played in that experience. This led to the emergence of Black feminist theorists, activists, and schol- ars who wanted to challenge the notion that the goals of racial equal- ity and women's rights should be kept separate. As Audre Lorde per- fectly stated, "I am a Black feminist. I mean I recognize that my power as well as my primary oppressions come as a result of my Blackness as well as my womanness, and therefore my struggles on both of these fronts are inseparable."[4] Inseparable, intertwined, and intersectional.

✹
WHAT IS MISOGYNOIR?

MISOGYNOIR, A concept originally defined by Black queer feminist Moya Bailey, is a term to describe a specific type of sexism that Black women face.[5] It stems from the term "misogyny": the hatred of women.[6] Misogynoir examines how race interacts with and compounds the impact of sexism and misogyny. Some examples include:

- ✹ **RACIAL DISPARITIES** for Black women in the health care system and increased maternal mortality rates.[7]
- ✹ **THE ANGRY BLACK WOMAN STEREOTYPE,** which contributes to the perception of Black women as threatening when they voice emotion.
- ✹ **THE STRONG BLACK WOMAN STEREOTYPE,** which discourages Black women from showing emotion.
- ✹ **THE HYPERSEXUALIZATION** of Black girls and women and the policing of their style choices. For example, natural hairstyles such as braids, locs, and Afros being banned in schools and workplaces.
- ✹ **THE DOUBLE STANDARD** when styles or features are perceived as "ghetto" when worn by Black women but praised when worn by white women.

Misogynoir explains the added level of specific discrimination that Black women face and how this discrimination permeates society. Misogynoir was very present during the women's rights movement and caused confusion at the intersections of race and feminism. In her book *Freedom Is a Constant Struggle,* civil rights activist Angela Davis explained, "Black feminism emerged as a theoretical and practical effort demonstrating that race, gender, and class are insepa-rable in the social worlds we inhabit. At the time of its emergence, Black women were frequently asked to choose whether the Black movement or the women's movement was most important. The response was that this was the wrong question."[8]

Being in the dominant racial group in society benefited white feminists to some extent during the women's rights movement. No matter how radical they were, they were allowed to publicly demon-strate without the same level of violence enacted on BIPOC, and they had the advantage of more visibility around their efforts. This isn't to say that their efforts should be minimized, but the purpose of this book is to raise awareness of unsung heroes, look beneath the surface, and reflect on missteps in social and environmental move-ments so that future movements can improve. With complete knowl-edge of our past, we have a better shot at improving the outcomes of our future.

Unfortunately, some early feminists had clear biases and chose to act only in their own best interests, disregarding the concerns of women of color and queer women because they felt that these top-ics weren't related, they didn't care, or they thought the inclusion of anti-racism or anti-homophobia would "complicate" the matter for white feminists. The prevailing attitude was that perhaps after *their own* liberation, they would create space for other people and causes.

It's confusing that early feminists, who believed deeply in the equality of men and women, had caveats as to who could achieve that liberation. To me, it's contradictory for a feminist to also hold racist, Islamophobic, anti-Semitic, homophobic, transphobic, and otherwise anti-liberation beliefs. However, humans are complicated, and lateral oppression—the concept of marginalized groups oppressing other marginalized groups—is very real. Sometimes the allure of power, however paltry, can cause otherwise oppressed people to contribute to the oppression of others.

With Black women's liberation seemingly an afterthought of women in the mainstream women's movement, it makes sense that Black feminists chose to create safer spaces so they could dive into the many aspects of their identities and fight for their own equality without waiting for white feminists to grant them permission. Instead, Black women created their own theories and framework that ultimately would benefit all women and would be more inclusive.

THE COMBAHEE RIVER COLLECTIVE

"If Black women were free, it would mean that everyone else would have to be free, since our freedom would necessitate the destruction of all the systems of oppression."

—Combahee River Collective statement[9]

LEADERSHIP WITHIN the U.S. civil rights movement was largely male, and the leaders of the women's rights movement were overwhelmingly middle-class and white. Black feminists found themselves at a crossroads. They lacked visibility and felt shut out of both movements. Even though they poured their emotional labor, hearts, and bodies into both causes because both were intertwined with their identities, they were left asking, Who will fight for us and where do we belong?

Twin sisters Barbara and Beverly Smith, Audre Lorde, Demita Frazier, Cheryl Clarke, Akasha Hull, Margo Okazawa-Rey, Chirlane McCray, and other Black feminist revolutionaries were tired of taking a back seat in their own liberation struggle. Together, they formed the Combahee River Collective in 1974, a small organization named after the Combahee River Raid in South Carolina, led by Harriet Tubman to liberate hundreds of enslaved people. The goals of the CRC were to combat capitalism, racism, homophobia, sexism, and more. The women wanted to dismantle several systems of oppression at once because to them, they were all interconnected.

The CRC, inspired by anticolonial and antiwar movements and the work of the Third World Women's Alliance, argued that the liberation of Black women would result in freedom for all people.[10] Black women were and are faced with racism, poverty, and sexism, and if Black women no longer bore the brunt of all these injustices, then everyone would benefit. This notion was revolutionary, because it is the opposite of white feminist ideologies that say that white women's liberation should come first and will eventually have a domino effect, and it is counter to some of the male-led civil rights organizations' positions that put Black women's interests second. The CRC believed that any oppressed group has the right to take up space and advocate for all aspects of their identity; as Black women, they were entitled to a political identity that centered around their Black womanhood, as any other oppressed person was entitled to a political identity that centered around their full personhood.[11] At the time, this was a radical response to being dismissed by other social movements that ignored the specific needs of Black women.

The CRC believed that oppressed people should be able to define their own political ideologies and organizations and advocate for their specific interests without silencing themselves; they termed this ability to self-determine "identity politics."[12] While the term has been misused since its inception, the intention was not to be exclusive, but to give oppressed people the right to advocate for their own self-interests and liberation. Black feminists did not view identity politics as a way to be separatists, but as a way to successfully unite and build stronger liberation movements.

"**We need to articulate the real class situation of persons who are not merely raceless, sexless workers, but for whom racial and sexual oppression are significant determinants in their working/ economic lives. Although we are in essential agreement with Marx's theory as it applied to the very specific economic relationships he analyzed, we know that his analysis must be extended further in order for us to understand our specific economic situation as Black women.**"

—Combahee River Collective statement

The CRC's stance was revolutionary because it expressed the complexity of overlapping identities and the sometimes double or triple marginalization that people with several oppressed identities faced. This multilayered approach to understanding oppression is the basis of intersectional theory.

❀ THE CHICANA IDENTITY

In this passage, Diandra Marizet, cofounder of Intersectional Environmentalist, unpacks intersectional feminism through the lens of the Chicana identity.

With growing up in the Southwest came a blend of many identities I learned were attributed to myself, my family, and our community. The ways I heard people like me referred to and how we referred to each other often went ill-defined by a telling of history that smudged the relevance of each term. I was referred to as Mexicana, Hispanic, Latina, Chicana, Tejana, or mestiza. Carrying an ambiguity around all these terms as a child created a confusion about who I was in the context of culture, ancestry, and home.

It was later in life that I learned some of these terms were created to root people like me in the struggles, pains, joys, and triumphs of my ancestors.

"Chicana," as an example, often refers to a Mexican American woman raised in the U.S. Being referred to as Chicano or Chicana was often held as derogatory; however, the term 'Chicana' was eventually embraced as an identity that acknowledged the unique ways Mexican American women experienced various forms of oppression. While Chicano men fought for sociopolitical equality in the 1960s and '70s, Mexican American women were still expected to maintain household work in a framework that didn't compensate them, protect them, or empower them. Much like the Chicano movement, second wave feminism also failed to address the racial and class struggles Mexican American women faced.

Being a Chicana was an intersectional form of feminism that acknowledged how gender, ethnicity, sexuality, class, race, and sociopolitical status played key roles in the oppression of Mexican American women and informed their fight for liberation. Both the Chicano and mainstream feminist movements wanted Chicanas to silence these overlapping issues to support the larger movements at hand.

In everyday practice, Chicanas aimed to push back against stereotypes that encouraged us to often be perceived as motherly, dutiful, and sexually pure—which would also contribute to issues around the oversexualization of young Mexican American women. The intercultural expectations placed on women like myself manifested into an ideology we refer to as "machismo," a way of thinking that aims to reinforce a male-dominated culture of leadership informed by male pride and a desire to be served by women. The imbalanced expectation to sacrifice oneself for their children left mothers experiencing machismo culture with little to no time for themselves and with little to no resources to fight the social, economic, and physical barriers preventing them from finding any form of liberation. Without appreciating the intersecting issues Mexican American women face, fighting back against this dynamic often led to Chicanas being accused of choosing gender over culture.

This ironic lack of consideration among Chicano and feminist "revolutionaries" led to prominent Mexican American women in the Chicano movement leaving to create their own rebel space. In the 1970s, Gloria Arellanes was the first woman to resign from the Brown Berets—a Mexican American group historically likened to the Black Panther Party. Despite making her way into leadership among the Brown Berets as minister of finance and correspondence, she expressed, "We have been treated as nothing, and not as revolutionary sisters." She was then followed by every woman in her segment and went on to organize efforts that would seek to liberate and empower Mexican American women.

This is a small sample of a history, unknown to me as a child, that I am now able to piece together so I can connect deeply to the legacies left behind for me and my community in hopes of proudly creating space for the complexities of our identities as they change and evolve through the continuation of this work.

—Diandra Marizet

KIMBERLÉ WILLIAMS CRENSHAW AND INTERSECTIONAL FEMINISM

BUILDING OFF the concept of interlocking systems of oppression and identity politics comes critical race theory and the theory of intersectionality, defined by Kimberlé Williams Crenshaw in 1989.

Crenshaw is a pioneer and leading voice in critical race theory, Black feminist legal theory, racism, and law, with over thirty years of research and advocacy on race and civil rights to her name. She is a graduate of Cornell University, Harvard University, and the University of Wisconsin and is a law professor at UCLA and Columbia. Her work has exposed several instances of structural inequality leading to the overcriminalization of Black children, such as the school-to-prison pipeline and the mistreatment of Black women in the criminal justice system. Critical race theory examines how race and identity intersect with power structures, like the legal system, and its foundational messaging began to emerge following the Civil Rights Movement in the '70s and carried on into the '80s and '90s. Its evolution can be credited to legal scholars including Derrick Bell, Alan Freeman, Richard Delgado, Cheryl Harris, Charles R. Lawrence III, Mari Matsuda, and Patricia J. Williams, as well as Crenshaw.

While these scholars' individual analyses may differ, there are two recurring arguments that are fundamental to the critical race theory movement:

1. **RACIST NOTIONS** of white superiority have resulted in systemic inequality, and the legal system upholds this system of power; and

2. **WE CAN TRANSFORM** the relationship between racism and power.[13]

25

Critical race theory (CRT) asserts that race is a social construct and that assigning societal values and authority to different races is what upholds systemic inequality. Contrary to polarized interpretations of both CRT and the term "identity politics," these theories are rooted in the desire to dismantle unequal power dynamics.

While critique is always warranted, the fear, hatred, polarization, and intentional distortion of self-protective theories created by Black women and other marginalized groups are a gaslighting tool used by those in power to silence dissent. Many of the visceral reactions to terms pioneered by Black women demonstrate what their creators endured, and still endure, to advocate for fair treatment.

Crenshaw's specific legal exploration of how discrimination against Black women impacts them negatively within the court system brought life to what we now know as intersectional theory. When reviewing the legal outcomes for Black women across a variety of cases, Crenshaw found that race, gender, and sex—not just one single aspect of their identity—all played a role in their sentences.

WHAT IS INTERSECTIONALITY?

"THE COMPLEX, cumulative way in which the effects of multiple forms of discrimination (such as racism, sexism, and classism) combine, overlap, or intersect especially in the experiences of marginalized individuals or groups.[14]

"Courts seem to think that race discrimination was what happened to all Black people across gender, and sex discrimination was what happened to all women, and if that is your framework, of course, what happens to Black women and other women of color is going to be difficult to see," said Kimberlé Williams Crenshaw in an interview with *Vox*. "Intersectionality was a prism to bring to light dynamics within discrimination law that weren't being appreciated by the courts."[15]

Crenshaw first explained intersectional theory in 1989 in her paper "Demarginalizing the Intersection of Race and Sex," which examined three court cases informed by sexism and racism simultaneously. She argued that the lack of consideration for both issues left Black women vulnerable and unprotected by the court.

In the 1976 case *DeGraffenreid v. General Motors,* the presiding judge ruled that Black women specifically could not be treated as a legally protected class even after only Black women were laid off in a round of firings in which white women and Black men kept their jobs.[16] While sex and race are protected classes, the combination of the two was a loophole in the legal system that led to the court absolving General Motors of this clear example of a combination of race and sex discrimination at play. General Motors was able to use the existing protected classes to cancel each other out. Crenshaw did not argue that a separate protected class needed to be created for those with intersectional identities, but that disregarding these intersections made Black women vulnerable targets for both racial and sex-based discrimination or judiciary dismissal.

The above is only a synopsis of Crenshaw's work, and I encourage you to look into her writings, live presentations, and workshops to gain further insights into her original intentions. Over time, intersectional theory has expanded to include the intersectional identities of other historically excluded and underrepresented groups and to consider other factors, like religion, sexual orientation, and nonbinary and trans identity. But it's important to understand its roots, its history, and the collective experiences of the Black women who laid the groundwork for this scholarship that has allowed many more of us to explain the complexities and multiple facets of our lives.

These theories and frameworks were put forth to bring about better outcomes and livelihoods for underrepresented and marginalized communities, but it's important to note that not everyone believes in systemic oppression, power structures, legal inequity, racial inequity, et cetera. Even people from underrepresented groups might not agree with these theories or support them. But I have found comfort in intersectional theory, and it has been a tool that has helped me advocate for myself, and I know it's done the same for others.

ECOFEMINISM

NOW THAT we better understand the origins of intersectional theory, let's look into how feminist movements and ideologies also led to the concept of intersectional environmentalism. Just as intersectional feminism looks at the significance of interlocking identities within the fight for gender equality, intersectional environmentalism examines the ways that interlocking identities, like race, class, sex, gender, and religion, impact environmental justice.

The exploration of the feminine in connection with nature dates back centuries to early philosophical, spiritual, or religious contexts and creation theories. In Greek mythology, Gaea (or Gaia) is seen as the first mother goddess and a personification of earth; before her, there was just Chaos.[17] Other cultures have their own versions of earth goddesses as well.[18]

* **BONO PEOPLE** of Ghana—Asase Ya (Asaase Yaa, Asaase Afua): The earth goddess of fertility, truth, and creation
* **MAYA—AKNA:** The goddess mother of Maya civilization who is the embodiment of fertility and childbirth
* **LEPCHA—BUNOO** (or Itbu-moo): The mother creator deity
* **MAORI—PAPATŪĀNUKU:** She is the land that gives birth to all things

✳ **NATIVE HAWAIIAN—PAPA** (Haumea and Ka Luahine): The Earth Mother

✳ **HUICHOL—TATEI YURIANAKA:** A fruitful Mother Earth

These early creation theories are largely responsible for some of the societal ideals we have surrounding women to this day. The connection between women and the earth, which is so deeply embedded in cultures around the world, laid the foundation for ecofeminism, a framework that explores the perceptions and treatment of women and nature in society (defined by French feminist Françoise d'Eaubonne in 1974).[19]

Ecofeminism is both a philosophy and a movement that exposes the dual oppressions of women and the environment as rooted in patriarchal structures. "[It] is a movement that sees a connection between the exploitation and degradation of the natural world and the subordination and oppression of women," writes Mary Mellor in *Feminism and Ecology*.[20] Ecofeminists argue that the treatment of women in society is a likely indicator of the treatment of the earth and vice versa; that because we live in a capitalist and patriarchal (or male-centered) society, the oppression of women and the destruction of nature are a natural consequence.

Ecofeminism was born out of the feminist and environmental movements of the 1970s and '80s, but many credit Ynestra King for popularizing the term with her 1987 *Nation* article "What Is Ecofeminism?" In this article, King asked readers to look inward and evaluate how their belief systems, as informed by society, contributed to the negative treatment of both women and the environment. This piece led to widespread awareness of the concept.

The Chipko movement, a forest conservation movement that originated in India in 1973, is regarded as one of the first ecofeminist demonstrations: more than two thousand women surrounded trees hand in hand to protest the destruction of nature.[21] In the years since, women have proceeded to play a pivotal role in environmental advocacy, continuing to honor the connection between the environment and the systemic inequalities faced by women.

By the late 1980s, two specific branches of ecofeminism had begun to develop: cultural ecofeminism and radical ecofeminism. Cultural ecofeminists often point to gender roles (like women being considered home carers and nurturers), biology (menstruation, breastfeeding, and childbirth), and spirituality and religion (goddess worship) as a basis for their belief that women share a strong connection with the earth.[22]

Radical ecofeminists argue that reinforcing gender roles upholds the patriarchy. Their practice is centered more around dismantling the patriarchy and the belief that women and nature are commodities that can be exploited. Radical ecofeminists argue against the negative portrayals of women and nature as "chaotic, emotional, and weak" and the reverse portrayals of men as "ordered and rational decision makers and leaders."[23] The fracture between cultural ecofeminism and radical ecofeminism also served to illuminate emerging concerns about the exclusion of women in the Global South and those of lower-income status, as well as LGBTQ+ and non-binary people.

Vandana Shiva, an Indian environmental activist, scholar, and writer, is one of the world's most prominent ecofeminists and is also a pillar of accountability within the movement. Shiva, who coauthored the book *Ecofeminism* in 1993 with German radical feminist Maria Mies, has raised awareness for what she calls subsistence feminism, which advocates that women's basic needs (clothing, food, shelter) be met in addition to more philosophical or societal needs that Western women typically press for (freedom, equality, liberation).[24] Shiva frequently emphasizes the need to include the concerns of non-Western women.

There are interlocking systems of oppression when it comes to feminism; without an intersectional approach, BIPOC, LGBTQ+, and other underrepresented women may be left out, erased, and not advocated for within Western interpretations of ecofeminism. Cultural ecofeminists' beliefs are deeply rooted in biology and gender roles, which can lead to the invalidation and exclusion of nonbinary, trans, and queer people from ecofeminism.

This is why to truly stand for justice for all women and the planet, ecofeminism must also be intersectional. Many practitioners do have an intersectional approach, whether they classify it as that or not. While ecofeminism was advanced by women of color like Vandana Shiva, my experience, as a student and an activist, is that it has often lacked representation of Black, Latinx, Indigenous, and Asian perspectives. At times, I have also witnessed ecofeminists appropriate Eastern religious and Indigenous traditions without proper credit, acknowledgment, or representation. It's important to make strides to be inclusive of all women and not just their ancestral theories, religious practices, and beliefs.

The desire to include vectors like class, race, sexual orientation, and religion within the eco conversation has led me to ponder what a more inclusive version of environmentalism, built on the foundations of Black feminism, ecofeminism, and intersectional theory, could look like.

INTERSECTIONAL ENVIRONMENTALISM

I DEFINE intersectional environmentalism (IE) as an inclusive approach to environmentalism that advocates for the protection of both people and the planet. IE argues that social and environmental justice are intertwined and that environmental advocacy that disregards this connection is harmful and incomplete. IE focuses on achieving climate justice, amplifying historically excluded voices, and approaching environmental education, policy, and activism with equity, inclusion, and restorative justice in mind.

I've always identified as an intersectional feminist, and I wanted to apply that framework to my environmental practice in order to ensure that my whole being was present in my environmental advocacy.

Both ecofeminism and intersectional environmentalism explore how the treatment and degradation of the earth is underscored by societal problems. But while ecofeminists focus primarily on how gender, sex, the patriarchy, and gender roles negatively impact the environment, intersectional environmentalism creates space for all social injustices and marginalized groups within the discourse. IE is informed by intersectional approaches to ecofeminism but also explores additional intersections of overlapping identities like religion, race, sexuality, age, ability, and class. Intersectional environmentalism acknowledges how social justice and environmentalism are intrinsically linked and how both must be considered to achieve environmental justice.

Intersectional environmentalism argues that the same systems of oppression that oppress people also oppress and degrade the planet. When a nation, such as one in the Global North, prioritizes extractive industries and profit over the planet, then it will likely also have interlinked social inequality. Degrading the planet also requires overlooking the negative impact on people, whether in the present or the near future.

IE also aims to create space for a more complete and inclusive retelling of environmental or natural history, one that embraces all cultural contributors to sustainability and environmentalism. Many Indigenous peoples worldwide have been better protectors and carers of the planet for thousands of years. Colonization and industrialization, rooted in capitalism, were direct attacks on both people and planet and are responsible for the climate crisis we are in. It is more important now than ever that we validate Indigenous wisdom, credit its origins, infuse it into environmental education, and fully embrace different cultural values that exist as the blueprint to what is now known as "sustainability," well before that terminology existed.

By embracing these traditions and giving them a platform and space within environmental education, we will allow historically excluded groups to teach their own stories and be leaders in the environmental movement. Just as ecosystems thrive on diversity and respect for resources, we should look toward diversity as an enhancement to environmental education and advocacy. And intersectional environmentalism wouldn't exist without the environmental justice movement and climate justice, which we will explore in Chapter 2: Environmental Justice: A Wider Lens.

Taking a closer look at historic events and movements helps shed light on the nuances of inequality that have long existed beneath the surface. Exposing these difficult realities isn't for the sake of pessimism or to discredit these causes. Instead, we can treat the exploration of nuance as a way to pave the way for more inclusive movements. Dismantling systems of oppression in the environmental movement begins with learning our history, in all its complexity, with the goal of creating a better legacy of environmentalism for all people and the planet.

I hope you approach this exploration with curiosity and adventure, because the journey of learning is never-ending and is even more beautiful when it's intersectional.

Q: What advice do you have for young Black girls who want to be in the climate space?

"Put down roots in places that reciprocate unconditional care. Black girls and women are constantly propped up as martyrs of superhuman strength, with the will and power to hold the weight of the world upon our shoulders. Yes, we are magic, but we also are human. Lean into your morality and prioritize spaces in this movement that validate not only your existence but your future. While we should never feel shamed for our capacity to love without return, we shouldn't have to give up our livelihoods in the process. There are so many people in this movement that are willing and excited to build a movement made in the image of all of us. Seek them out and grow in community with them."

—Wanjiku (Wawa) Gatheru, founder of Black Girl Environmentalist

THE IE PLEDGE BREAKOUT AND DISCUSSION:

I will stand in solidarity with Black, Indigenous, and POC communities and the planet.

We can learn from the work of Kimberlé Williams Crenshaw and the CRC and realize that we can stand in solidarity with oppressed people and the planet at the same time. The idea that we must prioritize one over the other often contributes to the oppression of people or disregard for the planet. If you are passionate about human rights, then environmental liberation is an intersecting issue. It is our responsibility as stewards of the earth to consider the impact that environmental harm has on the inhabitants of the earth, especially those who face the harshest realities.

So, how can you be an intersectional environmentalist and get started on your journey?

It's essential to own that systemic inequality exists within the climate movement. To right this wrong moving forward, intersectional environmentalists must acknowledge how many environmental protections haven't extended to BIPOC communities. This oversight leaves marginalized communities most vulnerable to the impacts of the climate crisis.

☀ CHAPTER DISCUSSION QUESTIONS:

DURING THE women's rights movement, Black feminism emerged due to splintering ideals and the lack of value that society placed on advocacy for those with overlapping identities (such as race and gender). We see this pattern play out not only with the separation of mainstream feminism and the creation of Black feminism/intersectional feminism, but with mainstream environmentalism and intersectional environmentalism. Why was this separation needed and what can future movements do to prevent this splintering from happening?

In this chapter, we explored feminism and environmentalism. What other movements or systems can intersectional theory be applied to? (Example: What would an intersectional approach to health care reform look like? Education reform?)

Terms created by people of color like "identity politics" and "intersectional theory" have been polarized and misused by being taken out of context. How can we combat misuse of these terms and ground them in their original meanings? How can we hold space for their original intentions while applying them to other systems?

CHAPTER 2

Environmental Justice: A Wider Lens

"Intersectional environmentalism is the lens. Environmental justice is the goal."

—Diandra Marizet, sustainability advocate and cofounder of Intersectional Environmentalist

AS WE established in Chapter 1, intersectionality is a framework that can be applied to environmentalism to accomplish the goal of environmental justice: the fair treatment of all people, regardless of identity, in regard to their environment. The concepts of climate justice, intersectional environmentalism, and environmentalism are not competing ideals: they are different expressions of the same quest for environmental liberation.

Knowledge is power and key in building a more equitable future. Through reflection and historical analysis, we can dismantle the flaws in our educational system, plant new seeds, unearth diverse stories of the past that are often left out of the conversation, and make environmental education more holistic, equitable, and representative. Let's begin here by taking a critical look at the history of environmental justice.

ENVIRONMENTAL JUSTICE, THE MOVEMENT AND PRACTICE

WHAT'S OFTEN left out of environmental history and education is how people of color have always been at the forefront of community advocacy. Even if they weren't as present at the first Earth Day or aren't as often seen summiting mountains in a national park, Black, Indigenous, and other communities of color are a part of environmental history in other very important ways. Whether it's activism for Indigenous sovereignty or Black and Brown communities confronting environmental hazards, there is a rich history of BIPOC environmental advocacy and a centuries-long legacy of fighting for justice.

The U.S. Environmental Protection Agency defines environmental justice as "the fair treatment and meaningful involvement of all people regardless of race, color, national origin, or income, with respect to the development, implementation, and enforcement of environmental laws, regulations, and policies."[1] The term "environmental justice" began to emerge in the 1980s, after both the civil rights and Earth Day movements; soon, environmental justice became a movement of its own.[2] We can turn to the "mother" and "father" of environmental justice to get started: Hazel M. Johnson and Dr. Robert Bullard.

Hazel M. Johnson was a Black environmental activist from the

South Side of Chicago, Illinois. After her husband passed away from lung cancer at the young age of forty-one, Johnson began to suspect an environmental connection.[3] In a short span of time following her husband's death in 1969, several others within her community, Altgeld Gardens, died from lung cancer. When a news report announced that Altgeld Gardens had some of the highest rates of cancer in all of Chicago, Johnson began to ask herself, Why would Altgeld Gardens, a community initially built for Black World War II veterans, have such abnormally high instances of cancer?[4]

When investigating the differences between primarily Black Altgeld Gardens and other Chicago neighborhoods, Johnson found that Altgeld Gardens bore a tremendously disproportionate environmental hazard burden. Just one-third of a square mile contained fifty landfills, hundreds of toxic waste sites, and 250 leaking underground storage tanks.[5] The housing development had been built in the 1940s, constructed on an old car company dump with approval from the Chicago Housing Authority—despite the city's awareness of high asbestos levels. Toxic waste and pollution completely surrounded and engulfed the community in a "toxic doughnut" (a term Johnson coined to describe the phenomena of communities that were placed in the center of environmental injustice).[6]

While some may have overlooked the increased placement of toxic waste facilities in Black communities and deemed the occurrence *coincidental*, Johnson fought her entire career to prove that it was intentional. All across the United States, Black and low-income communities were plagued with environmental hazards that impacted the health of residents and often resulted in illness, worsened quality of life, and death. Johnson fought for legislators and community members to recognize the racism at play and its serious consequences on health and the environment.

"For so long, environmental activism has been primarily a white, middle-class issue, far removed from the daily reality of inner-city life," Johnson told the *Chicago Tribune* in 1955.[7] "It's all very well to embrace saving the rain forests and conserving endangered animal species, but such global initiatives don't even begin to impact communities inhabited by people of color."

Johnson's work was mostly carried out through her organization, People for Community Recovery (PCR), established in 1979, and she was a leading voice in the creation of the seventeen Principles of Environmental Justice, which she presented to Congress in 1993. Johnson's testimony, alongside that of other environmental activists, led to President Bill Clinton's executive order 12898 in 1994, which focused on environmental injustice.[8]

❁ THE SEVENTEEN PRINCIPLES OF ENVIRONMENTAL JUSTICE 1991[9]

Delegates to the First National People of Color Environmental Leadership Summit held on October 24–27, 1991, in Washington, DC, drafted and adopted these seventeen principles of Environmental Justice.

WE, THE PEOPLE OF COLOR gathered together at this multinational People of Color Environmental Leadership Summit, to begin to build a national and international movement of all peoples of color to fight the destruction and taking of our lands and communities, do hereby reestablish our spiritual interdependence to the sacredness of our Mother Earth; to respect and celebrate each of our cultures, languages, and beliefs about the natural world and our roles in healing ourselves; to ensure environmental justice; to promote economic alternatives which would contribute to the development of environmentally safe livelihoods; and to secure our political, economic, and cultural liberation that has been denied for over five hundred years of colonization and oppression, resulting in the poisoning of our communities and land and the genocide of our peoples, do affirm and adopt these Principles of Environmental Justice:

1. **ENVIRONMENTAL JUSTICE AFFIRMS** the sacredness of Mother Earth, ecological unity and the interdependence of all species, and the right to be free from ecological destruction.

2. **ENVIRONMENTAL JUSTICE DEMANDS** that public policy be based on mutual respect and justice for all peoples, free from any form of discrimination or bias.

3. **ENVIRONMENTAL JUSTICE MANDATES** the right to ethical, balanced, and responsible uses of land and renewable resources in the interest of a sustainable planet for humans and other living things.

4. **ENVIRONMENTAL JUSTICE CALLS** for universal protection from nuclear testing, extraction, production, and disposal of toxic/hazardous wastes and poisons and nuclear testing that threaten the fundamental right to clean air, land, water, and food.

5. **ENVIRONMENTAL JUSTICE AFFIRMS** the fundamental right to political, economic, cultural, and environmental self-determination of all peoples.

6. **ENVIRONMENTAL JUSTICE DEMANDS** the cessation of the production of all toxins, hazardous wastes, and radioactive materials, and that all past and current producers be held strictly accountable to the people for detoxification and the containment at the point of production.

7. **ENVIRONMENTAL JUSTICE DEMANDS** the right to participate as equal partners at every level of decision-making, including needs assessment, planning, implementation, enforcement, and evaluation.

8. **ENVIRONMENTAL JUSTICE AFFIRMS** the right of all workers to a safe and healthy work environment without being forced to choose between an unsafe livelihood and unemployment. It also affirms the right of those who work at home to be free from environmental hazards.

9. **ENVIRONMENTAL JUSTICE PROTECTS** the right of victims of environmental injustice to receive full compensation and reparations for damages as well as quality health care.

10. **ENVIRONMENTAL JUSTICE CONSIDERS** governmental acts of environmental injustice a violation of international law, the Universal Declaration on Human Rights, and the United Nations Convention on Genocide.

11. **ENVIRONMENTAL JUSTICE MUST** recognize a special legal and natural relationship of Native Peoples to the U.S. government through treaties, agreements, compacts, and covenants affirming sovereignty and self-determination.

12. **ENVIRONMENTAL JUSTICE AFFIRMS** the need for urban and rural ecological policies to clean up and rebuild our cities and rural areas in balance with nature, honoring the cultural integrity of all our communities, and providing fair access for all to the full range of resources.

13. **ENVIRONMENTAL JUSTICE CALLS** for the strict enforcement of principles of informed consent, and a halt to the testing of experimental reproductive and medi-

cal procedures and vaccinations on people of color.

14. **ENVIRONMENTAL JUSTICE OPPOSES** the destructive operations of multinational corporations.

15. **ENVIRONMENTAL JUSTICE OPPOSES** military occupation, repression, and exploitation of lands, peoples and cultures, and other life-forms.

16. **ENVIRONMENTAL JUSTICE CALLS** for the education of present and future generations which emphasizes social and environmental issues, based on our experience and an appreciation of our diverse cultural perspectives.

17. **ENVIRONMENTAL JUSTICE REQUIRES** that we, as individuals, make personal and consumer choices to consume as little of Mother Earth's resources and to produce as little waste as possible; and make the conscious decision to challenge and reprioritize our lifestyles to ensure the health of the natural world for present and future generations.

The Proceedings of the First National People of Color Environmental Leadership Summit are available from the United Church of Christ Commission for Racial Justice.

Hazel M. Johnson's work helped lay the groundwork for climate justice around the world, as well as for an intersectional approach to environmentalism. It's important to also note that she was met with sexism, racism, and classism throughout her career, and has been omitted from many environmental textbooks. As intersectional environmentalists, we are now presented with the opportunity to re-create what environmental education should look like, and we can work together to honor stories like Johnson's to ensure that her legacy, and those of other BIPOC environmentalists, lives on.

Another pivotal voice in environmental justice history is its "father," as he's often dubbed, Dr. Robert Bullard. Bullard grew up in Elba, Alabama, a Black neighborhood, and attended high school during the height of the civil rights movement in the 1960s.[10] His teachers deviated from the approved curriculum and taught students about civil rights, which had a lasting impact on Bullard's life and commitment to justice.

After graduating from the prominent, historically Black university Alabama A&M with a B.S. in government, Bullard joined the United States Marine Corps, was deployed in 1970, and served for two years.[11] He then attended Clark Atlanta University, earning a master's in sociology in 1972, and received a PhD in sociology from Iowa State University in 1976. Two years later, Bullard was asked to conduct research that would forever alter his life and lead him down the path toward environmental justice.

Dr. Bullard's wife, attorney Linda McKeever Bullard, was working on a landfill placement case, representing Margaret Bean and other Houston residents in the Northwood Manor neighborhood who were trying to contest the plan. Northwood Manor was an eyebrow-raising choice for a landfill because it was a middle-class and suburban neighborhood. The only thing that differentiated it from other middle-class neighborhoods in the area was that it was 82 percent Black.[12] Recognizing this distinction, Linda McKeever Bullard filed a lawsuit, *Bean v. Southwestern Waste Management, Inc.,* the first case of its kind, claiming that the location selection of toxic waste facilities was violating its residents' civil rights.[13] To help prove her assumption that the placement was linked to racial discrimination, Dr. Bullard was called as an expert witness. During this time, he conducted a study to explore the link between toxic waste site placement and race.

Dr. Bullard's research found that race had been a driving factor in the location of toxic waste sites. The *Bean v. Southwestern Waste Management, Inc.* lawsuit took place in Houston, where even though Black residents represented only 25 percent of the population, Black neighborhoods had a disproportionately high number of waste disposal sites.[14] In 1979, Dr. Bullard wrote "Solid Waste Sites and the Black Houston Community," one of the first studies to demonstrate the link between toxic waste locations and race.

Shortly after, he published his first book, *Dumping in Dixie: Race, Class, and Environmental Quality,* which established the research-backed conclusion that Black communities in the southern United States had been targeted for the placement of landfills and incinerators, lead smelters, petrochemical plants, and other toxic facilities.[15] Even though the lawsuit ruled in favor of the defendant, Southwestern Waste Management Corp., in *Bean v. Southwestern Waste Management, Inc.,* Dr. Bullard's research became foundational for a new field of environmental justice, and a lifetime of advocacy was set in motion.

Dr. Bullard helped plan the First National People of Color Environmental Leadership Summit in 1991, which was the birthplace of the seventeen Principles of Environmental Justice provided earlier in this chapter. Since then, Dr. Bullard has gone on to publish over a dozen books on environmental justice, and he has fought tirelessly to elevate environmental justice in environmental education and policy.

In his own words, environmental justice can be defined as a concept that "embraces the principles that all communities, all people, are entitled to equal protection of our environmental laws, health laws, housing laws, transportation laws, and civil rights laws." He continues,

"If we talk about the major elements of environmental justice, it includes equal enforcement of laws and regulations, identifying and eliminating discriminatory practices and policies. Whether those policies and practices are intended or unintended doesn't matter. If there are impacts that are regressive, that are negative, that fall heaviest on a certain population, and if we can eliminate those effects, we should do it."

—Dr. Robert Bullard, quote from transcript of his live presentation "Environmental Justice: Strategies for Creating Healthy and Sustainable Communities," delivered at Mercer Law School[16]

Dr. Bullard's point on intention versus impact is crucial. Even if early environmentalists didn't intend to contribute to systemic racial and economic injustice, loopholes in environmental policy certainly did. And these loopholes and oversights—which led to everything from contaminated drinking water to farmworker exposure to toxic pesticides—had long-lasting impacts on the health and safety of people globally. Thankfully, by looking to the past and fully acknowledging these oversights, we have the opportunity to create a more accountable future.

Q: What is environmental liberation and why is it important to achieving environmental justice?

"As a part of the founding team for Generation Green, I coined the term 'environmental liberation' to name the ideological framework that we've developed as an organization that achieves Black liberation, climate justice, and environmental justice as one—through diasporic organizing and community building. Environmental liberation (EL) critically analyzes the injustices in the environment(s) of the Black experience that stem from colonialism, racial capitalism, and white supremacy. Environmental liberation has an Afrocentric lens and sees Blackness through the lens of decolonial border thinking. It centers both Afro-Indigeneity and ancestral ways of knowing alongside Afro-futuristic visions of Black people thriving all throughout the Black diaspora. Environmental liberation transcends the confines of the bureaucratic neoliberal state 'justice' by identifying the North Star of the EL movement: making sure that Black people can be liberated and thrive in their environments.

"Advocating for 'justice' becomes tricky when you are not meaningfully engaged in or in control of the processes and systems that distribute environmental burdens and assets. EL pushes the need for equity further by seeking liberation and restitution from the systems and entities that have created environments of oppression, extraction, exploitation, and pollution for Black people and our marginalized allies."

—Ayana Albertini-Fleurant, co–executive director and director of policy and programming at Generation Green

THE ENVIRONMENTAL + ENVIRONMENTAL JUSTICE MOVEMENTS

WE OWE the civil rights movements of Black, Indigenous, Latinx, Pacific Islander, people of color, and Asian communities a lot of praise for paving the way for the environmental movements that we have today. Their movements were often intersectional in nature because these peoples were fighting for their right to live free of discrimination and harassment and to have equal access to an opportunity for a safe and healthy life. If you're wondering, "Isn't the American civil rights movement all about race and racial equality?," the answer is yes, but racial equality also includes environmental equality, economic opportunity, health care access, educational reform, and so on. Civil rights movements are multifaceted because several systems of oppression are connected to race. We have to find the nuance and overlapping ideals of different social movements in order to find the roots of intersectional environmentalism.

In the 1960s, while civil rights leaders were advocating for an end to racial segregation and discrimination, they were also raising awareness about the environmental and public health concerns that plagued their communities.

In 1968, Black sanitation workers in Memphis, Tennessee, went on strike to protest dangerous working conditions and lack of adequate pay. According to the Environmental Protection Agency, the Memphis sanitation strikes were the first time Black Americans mobilized a "national, broad-based group to oppose what they considered environmental injustice"; together, with the help of Dr. Martin Luther King Jr., they advocated for both worker safety and fair compensation—an intersection of health, environmental, racial, and economic justice.[17]

The following year, in 1969, Indigenous rights activists also changed history, with a nineteen-month occupation of Alcatraz Island in San Francisco, California, that garnered global attention. During their protest, activists demanded that Alcatraz be returned to Indigenous peoples and that the U.S. government implement restorative justice programs to improve infrastructure and sanitation facilities, ensure fresh running water, enrich the soil, and more.[18] Their demands were multifaceted and intersectional and addressed broken treaties and broken promises and highlighted the continual mistreatment and violence faced by Indigenous peoples.

"It's easy to pass off the Alcatraz event as largely symbolic, but the truth is, the spirit and dream of Alcatraz never died; it simply found its way to other fights," wrote Benjamin and Peter Bratt, Quechua natives from Peru who lived on Alcatraz during the occupation.[19] "Native sovereignty, repatriation, environmental justice, the struggle for basic human rights—these are the issues Native people were fighting for then, and are the same things we are fighting for today." This was one of many occupation efforts of Indigenous activists to reclaim and restore their land and culture and to advocate for total sovereignty.

The Warren County, North Carolina, sit-in is often referenced as the cornerstone case that started the environmental justice movement of the 1980s (which we'll get to shortly). However, it's important to examine what exactly happened between the 1968 Memphis sanitation strikes, the 1969 Indigenous occupation of Alcatraz, and the 1982 Warren County sit-in to understand why an intersectional approach to environmentalism is essential.

What exactly happened in the decade between the end of the civil rights movement and the emergence of the environmental justice movement? If the Earth Day movement happened in the 1970s, why would we even need an environmental justice movement? Because the concerns of people of color were not adequately addressed during the Earth Day movement and because people of color had to perform additional emotional labor to advocate for correcting environmental injustice impacting their communities. The events between 1969 and 1982 illustrate why an intersectional approach to environmentalism is essential to protecting all people equally.

Shortly after Dr. Martin Luther King Jr. spoke to the Memphis sanitation strikers in 1968, he was assassinated. This was a national tragedy, and it was also a major setback for environmental justice. Just as civil rights activists had begun to speak up against environmental injustices, a beloved leader was lost, followed by several other prominent Black leaders. As many civil rights activists and Black citizens grieved, a largely white environmental movement began to sweep the United States. These environmentalists took note of the tactics used by civil rights protesters, like sit-ins and marches, and began to use those strategies to spread awareness about conservation, pollution, toxic waste, and more.

The movement finally ignited in 1969, when disturbing images of Cleveland, Ohio's Cuyahoga River engulfed in flames (yes, a body of water with fire raging on top of it!) were published in *Time* magazine; the United States was shocked and wanted to know more.[20] The river fire, caused by extremely flammable oil, gas, and toxic waste dumped into waterways, was far from anomalous during this time period, but with this one article, the nation came face-to-face with what a world on fire could look like if policies didn't adequately protect the planet.[21]

In response, millions took to the streets, protesting and pressuring politicians to implement federal environmental policies. This collective action led to the largest environmental demonstration in history, on April 22, 1970: Earth Day, in which twenty million Americans called for a drastic improvement in environmental policy.[22] The first Earth Day was a spectacular feat, with gatherings and activities across the world. However, even though it was inspired by and occurred in close proximity with the civil rights movement and civil rights efforts of Chicano and Indigenous activists, it was largely white led and attended.[23] Which brings us to the question, What is the impact of having large-scale environmental movements that mostly exclude the voices of the underrepresented and people of color?

Chicano movement activist Arturo Sandoval, founder of the Center of Southwest Culture, was on the organizing team of the first national Earth Day in 1970 and has since spent his life answering that very question. When reflecting on his involvement with Earth Day in an interview with Bioneers.org decades later, he said, "As a Chicano, I was definitely a fish out of water. Basically, I did feel clear class differentials. I felt the class difference, and I did feel marginalized. Generally, Chicano activists and Black activists were not drawn to the first Earth Day because they were so deeply engaged in their own local issues. They were fighting for survival."[24]

Activists like Cesar Chavez and Dolores Huerta were also fighting in the 1960s and '70s for Latinx families to have safer environments. Their activism shouldn't have been considered separate from the Earth Day movement, but it was. Not only did their work contribute to the overall movement, but their efforts helped lead to the ban on the use of harmful pesticides that impacted farmworker safety and increased awareness of environmental justice within the Latinx community. However, because of racism, xenophobia (fear of immigrants), and classism, these activists were excluded.

Q: Who are some of the heroes that inspired you to found Latino Outdoors and advocate for Latinx representation in the outdoors?

"There are many unnamed elders and heroes in this work, along with contemporary peers. To do them justice would be to have a LONG and ongoing list. Still, some names to start include:

- ✿ YNÉS ENRIQUETTA JULIETTA MEXÍA
- ✿ RALPH ABASCAL
- ✿ DOLORES HUERTA
- ✿ EMMA TENAYUCA
- ✿ ARTURO SANDOVAL
- ✿ JUAN MARTINEZ
- ✿ OMAR GALLARDO
- ✿ MARCE GUTIÉRREZ-GRAUDIŅŠ

"All of the Latino Outdoors leaders, past and present."

—José González, founder and director emeritus of Latino Outdoors

According to Arturo Sandoval, "After Earth Day, there was a succession of a lot of national federal legislation—maybe twenty or thirty federal acts—enacted specifically to protect the environment, clean air and water acts. That success in many ways ended up causing a long-term issue for environmental groups. It led them to believe that being primarily composed of white middle-class and upper middle-class citizens was enough to get the job done, that they did not need to change their approach or their tactics. Nor did they need to reach out to working people, to rural people, to Chicanos and Mexicanos and African Americans. They really never made it a fundamental value of their work or strategy to try to include these groups. We're paying the price for that now."[25]

Here's what he means: although the Earth Day movement led to the creation of the Environmental Protection Agency and the passage of several prominent federal environmental laws, like the Clean Air Act (CAA) and the Clean Water Act, it can be argued that these laws did not equally protect all Americans. While primarily white communities in the U.S. saw a 70 percent reduction in air pollution after the CAA was passed, low-income and Black, Indigenous, Asian, Pacific Islander, and Latinx communities were seemingly left out of the parameters of protection outlined in these laws.[26] In fact, some of the new environmental legislation passed in the 1970s directly diverted toxic waste into Black, Brown, and low-income communities. This exclusion and unethical treatment led to the emergence of the environmental justice movement in the 1980s.

One piece of legislation passed after the Earth Day movement was the 1976 Resource Conservation and Recovery Act (RCRA), which created guidelines for the proper disposal and management of toxic waste. This legislation should have ensured that toxic waste was placed far away from largely populated communities, but this wasn't the case with Warren County, North Carolina. Even though this site did not meet EPA guidelines for hazardous waste landfills, in 1982, the state of North Carolina selected Warren County as the location for the disposal of polychlorinated biphenyl–contaminated soil, a known carcinogen.[27] The problem? Warren County was not a "proper" disposal site: it was the home of a very populated Black community. This inconvenient fact was just out of sight, out of mind for the primarily white and middle-class environmentalists who fought for the passage of the environmental regulations meant to protect all Americans from harm.

Black activists and allies mobilized in several public demonstrations and sit-ins to try to oppose the toxic landfill in Warren County, emphasizing the civil rights violations of repeatedly placing toxic waste sites in Black communities. During the sit-ins, five hundred demonstrators and activists were arrested, and unfortunately, the landfill construction continued.[28] However, these demonstrations prompted the U.S. Congress to task the United States Government Accountability Office (GAO) with investigating. The GAO's 1983 report "Siting of Hazardous Waste Landfills and Their Correlation with Racial and Economic Status" concluded that in three out of the four primary toxic landfill sites, the surrounding communities were Black, with over 26 percent of residents living below the poverty line.[29] This was one of the first government-issued studies that presented clear data-driven findings of environmental racism.

Several environmental justice organizations and coalitions formed in response to these findings, including the Indigenous Environmental Network, West Harlem Environmental Action, and the Southwest Network for Environmental and Economic Justice. In the following decade, these groups secured funding for communal environmental initiatives, blocked environmentally harmful projects (like landfills, toxic sites, and pipelines), and more.

Startlingly, as of 2019, race is still *the number one* indicator of where toxic waste facilities are located in the U.S. According to Paul Mohai, an environmental justice expert and professor at the University of Michigan, even when socioeconomic factors are similar across white and non-white communities, the community of color is still more likely to be near environmental hazards.[30] The fight for environmental justice remains urgent, even more so as we face the climate crisis.

We may not be able to change the past, but we can reflect upon and learn from history. We are still bearing the lasting impacts of excluding communities of color in large-scale environmental movements due to laws that overlook and harm communities of color. We must remedy the missed opportunities of the 1960s and '70s by taking action together and uniting as one force for change.

History often repeats itself, and large civil rights and climate movements have emerged again. In 2013, following the 2012 murder of Trayvon Martin, an unarmed Black teenager who was racially profiled and confronted while walking to a family friend's house, activists Alicia Garza, Patrisse Cullors, and Opal Tometi created the phrase and hashtag Black Lives Matter. Their campaign grew into a global movement following the deaths of even more unarmed Black men and women killed by excessive force, galvanizing millions of protesters over the years in the largest civil rights movement of the twenty-first century. LANDBACK, a movement to reclaim everything stolen from Indigenous peoples—land, language, ceremony, medicines, and kinship—is growing. The Stop Asian Hate movement, sparked by a global increase in discrimination and violence against Asian people, is gaining momentum and resulting in policy shifts (such as an anti-Asian hate crimes bill).

At the same time, a new generation of climate activists are emerging all across the globe. The Youth Strike for Climate, also known as Fridays for Future, began in 2018 after Swedish youth activist Greta Thunberg staged a protest in front of the Swedish parliament holding a sign that read "Skolstrejk för klimatet" (School Strike for Climate). Her actions, along with those of several other brave students, resulted in an international movement of students of various ages that demonstrated and walked out of Friday classes to demand climate action, a transition to renewable energy, and a commitment to stopping the climate crisis. By 2019, over one million demonstrators, primarily students, across 150 countries had participated in the protests.

From the People's Climate Movement, Extinction Rebellion, and Fridays for Future to March for Science, millions globally have publicly demonstrated and advocated for major environmental policy shifts that would protect the future of the planet. Environmental justice protests like the Dakota Access Pipeline protests and Mauna Kea protests—led by Indigenous activists—have also attracted global attention as they call for greater inclusion in environmental policy and demand considerations for Indigenous peoples and their livelihoods.

Social justice action and environmental advocacy are again aligning side by side as they did during the civil rights and Earth Day movements, and once again we run the risk of undermining both movements by keeping them separate.

What if, instead, we gathered under a common goal for both social and environmental justice? This enormous gathering power could be an even larger force if we realized through intersectional environmentalism that climate justice and social justice are inextricably linked and interconnected. We've seen how separating the very real impacts of racial and economic inequalities from environmental movements weakens both causes, and we'll look closer at the data in the next chapter.

THE IE PLEDGE BREAKOUT AND DISCUSSION:

I will not ignore the intersections of environmentalism and social justice.

To dismantle systems of oppression in the environmental movement, the first step is acknowledging the intersections that environmental justice advocates have been highlighting for decades! Environmental justice and intersectional environmentalism should no longer exist only outside the confines of traditional environmental education and must be mandatory in order to ensure inclusivity and more representative climate action and solutions.

CHAPTER DISCUSSION QUESTIONS:

✳ **WHAT ARE** the environmental injustices facing my local community?

  ✳ The U.S. Environmental Protection Agency has an Environmental Justice in Your Community tool on its website that expands on environmental injustices in ten regions in the U.S., including ten tribal nations.

✳ **IS MY** community impacted by food apartheid, higher air or water pollution, or a toxic doughnut?

✳ **IS MY** town racially segregated?

✳ **IS THERE** significant green space in my community? What about neighboring cities?

✳ **WHEN I** visit the green spaces in my community, are they free and open to the public?

✳ **DOES MY** local school system offer classes on environmental justice?

✳ **DO I** view the climate crisis as a hypothetical future? Do I acknowledge the present realities of the environmental justice crisis that BIPOC and low-income communities face? Have I been dismissive of climate justice in the past?

IF YOU'RE AN ENVIRONMENTAL SCIENCE OR STUDIES STUDENT OR EDUCATOR:

* **ARE THERE** classes taught by BIPOC, LGBTQ+, and disabled professors at my learning institution?

* **IF THERE** are no such classes offered, how can I take my learning outside the classroom to ensure that I'm broadening my education by creating space to learn from diverse environmental perspectives?

* **(IF YOU** are a student:) Can I make a conscious effort to take a class taught from a perspective outside my own?

* **(IF YOU** are a BIPOC student looking to find community:) How can I find community online or in person as well as safe and supportive spaces?

    * There are organizations and platforms like Black Girl Environmentalist, Generation Green, Latino Outdoors, Hike Clerb, Outdoor Afro, Melanin Base Camp, Indigenous Women Hike, and more.

CHAPTER 3

Unpacking Privilege

CONVERSATIONS SURROUNDING race, culture, religion, gender identity, and sexuality are becoming more common in our everyday lives. Some people opt out of these conversations because they fear discomfort, anger, and conflict; however, this doesn't have to be the case. The more we talk about our identities and the ways they influence how we experience the world, the better we can understand how they're connected to both the privileges and prejudices we might experience.

The truth is, ignoring our differences doesn't stop discrimination or lead to systemic change. While conversations about privilege aren't always welcome, even in environmental spaces, the alternative—denial, defensiveness, or dismissiveness—can further perpetuate harm and make it more difficult to undo unjust policies that disproportionately impact people based on their race, socioeconomic status, location, or other aspects of identity. Hopefully one day we will live in a society where everyone has equal opportunity and access to a safe and healthy environment. In the meantime, it's crucial to understand and unpack privilege so we can get closer to a greener and more equitable future for all.

WHAT IS PRIVILEGE?

WE ALL have parts of our identities that shape how we relate to the world and how the world relates to us. The smallest things, from freckles on our faces to the tones of our voices, can influence how we're perceived by others and ultimately how they might treat us. These personal perceptions can lead to an accumulation of assumptions that become societal perceptions or biases that can be positive, neutral, or negative. Privilege is a set of unearned advantages, positive perceptions, and outcomes based on identity.

Society, the media, and cultural norms help shape the biases, stereotypes, and assumptions that are tied to larger aspects of our identities like race, sexuality, gender, ability, age, and so on. Some identity groups unequally experience more positive assumptions, while others are on the receiving end of neutral or negative assumptions. These assumptions can lead to biases that cause an identity aspect—a piece of someone's identity—to be favored or valued more than other identity aspects. When an identity aspect is assigned a higher value in a society, those who possess it are more likely to hold power both individually and as a group. This is known as privilege.

✳

WHAT IS AN IDENTITY ASPECT?

I USE the term "identity aspect" to explain components of some-one's overall identity. The "big eight" identities comprise eight iden-tity aspects, many of which are socially constructed, that help us understand who we are and also play a role in how we are perceived by others. The big eight identities are age, ability, race, ethnicity, gender, sexual orientation, socioeconomic status, and religion.[1]

✳

WHAT IS A SOCIAL CONSTRUCT?

A SOCIAL construct is an idea pertaining to interpersonal relationships and societal norms that has been created and accepted by the mem-bers of a society.[2] Social constructs do not always have a factual basis and can shift depending on the society and culture. Social constructs are beliefs that members of a society hold and assign meaning and value to. For example, a common argument is that race is a social construct. This doesn't mean that there aren't different ethnicities of people, but that assigning value and meaning to different racial groups in a society is a social construct. When people use racism as a justification for the mistreatment of other people, they are playing off a social construct that race inherently makes humans different from one another—when there is no factual or scientific basis for this. Stereotypes are born out of social constructs.

Before the term "privilege" made its way into academia, W.E.B. Du Bois wrote about a similar concept that he called "psychological wage" in his 1935 book *Black Reconstruction in America*.[3] He felt that even poor white Americans were granted advantages in society that weren't given to Black Americans. These advantages ranged from positive biases to better treatment in the criminal justice system and more public acceptance solely because of their race.[4] He reflected,

"It must be remembered that the white group of laborers, while they received a low wage, were compensated in part by a sort of public and psychological wage. They were given public deference and titles of courtesy because they were white. They were admitted freely with all classes of white people to public functions, public parks, and the best schools. The police were drawn from their ranks, and the courts, dependent on their votes, treated them with such leniency as to encourage lawlessness. Their vote selected public officials, and while this had small effect upon the economic situation, it had great effect upon their personal treatment and the deference shown them. White schoolhouses were the best in the community, and conspicuously placed, and they cost anywhere from twice to ten times as much per capita as the colored schools. The newspapers specialized on news that flattered the poor whites and almost utterly ignored the Negro except in crime and ridicule."[5]

In the years following W.E.B. Du Bois's writings, many other civil rights activists and scholars also spoke about unearned societal advantages and disadvantages tied to race. In 1988, Peggy McIntosh, a women's studies scholar at Wellesley College, was one of the first to write about privilege in a social justice context in her article "White Privilege and Male Privilege: A Personal Account of Coming to See Correspondences Through Work in

Women's Studies." The article contained forty-six examples of what she viewed as unearned societal privileges,[6] including the ability to:

- ✴ **BE REASONABLY SURE** that my neighbors in such a location will be neutral or pleasant to me.
- ✴ **GO SHOPPING ALONE** most of the time, fairly well assured that I will not be followed or harassed by store detectives.
- ✴ **NOT HAVE TO** educate our children to be aware of systemic racism for their own daily physical protection.
- ✴ **BE REASONABLY SURE** that if I ask to talk to "the person in charge," I will be facing a person of my race.

The examples ranged from stereotypes she would likely never face due to her race to positive assumptions she was granted in society based on her whiteness alone. When these individual advantages are multiplied by thousands of people within a society, they amount to systemic advantages and eventually determine who holds more power.

More recently, the 2020 *New York Times* report "Faces of Power" did a comprehensive review of the identities of nine hundred executives and prominent officials in the U.S. The reporters uncovered that only 20 percent identified as persons of color.[7] They surveyed executives at the highest-valued companies, the heads of the country's top twenty-five universities, directors of major news organizations, members of the U.S. Supreme Court, and other influential positions of leadership across the nation. While 40 percent of people in the U.S. identify as people of color, 80 percent of the "faces of power" were white and largely male.[8] This is an example of one identity aspect group holding a disproportionate amount of decision-making power; even though white men were 31 percent of the U.S. population in 2014, they held 65 percent of all elected offices.[9] During the survey time period from 2010 to 2019, the U.S. population was 48.9 percent male and 51.1 percent female, with 7.43 million more women.[10]

The demographics of the U.S. are changing rapidly, and people of color are projected to collectively become a majority by 2045; even so, there are still systemic barriers and obstacles tied to privilege that contribute to inequality.[11] Those in power determine the delegation of resources and the quality and availability of those resources.

LET'S TAKE A LOOK AT THE DATA:

- **THE WAGE GAP:** In 2018, the average Black worker earned only 62 percent of what the average white worker made, despite an increase in college degrees and higher education among both Black and white Americans.[12] When examined through an intersectional lens, women of color earned less in comparison, and those who were LGBTQ+ earned even less.

- **UPWARD MOBILITY:** White children from low-income families are more likely than Black children from low-income families to move into a higher income bracket in their lifetimes.[13] Even when Black and Indigenous peoples in the U.S. are born into higher income brackets, they are almost as likely to fall into a lower income bracket throughout their lifetimes as they are to exceed or stay in the income bracket of their parents.[14]

- **EDUCATION:** BIPOC schools receive $23 billion less in funding than primarily white schools, which leads to gaps in education. Students of color have to overcome more barriers to have access to AP classes and college preparation resources. "For every student enrolled, the average non-white school district receives $2,226 less than a white school district," according to a 2019 report from the nonprofit EdBuild.[15]

* **FINANCIAL ASSISTANCE:** Even though home loan discrimination is illegal in the U.S., Black, Latinx, and Asian mortgage loan applicants are more likely to be denied. This has led to a steep difference in home ownership along racial lines: 73.7 percent for whites, 48.9 percent for Latinx, and 44 percent for Black Americans, affecting the potential for long-term wealth growth and stability.[16]

* **CRIMINAL JUSTICE:** Although usage rates are similar, Black Americans are more likely to be arrested and jailed for drug-related charges. In 2018, Black Americans were 3.6 times more likely to be arrested on marijuana charges.[17] Black defendants are denied bail at higher rates and are more likely to receive harsher sentences than white defendants for the same crime.[18]

These are just a few examples of how identity aspects are tied to systemic advantages and disadvantages. The differences in our identities have led to struggles for power throughout history, from the civil rights and disability justice movements to the cross-political conflict that continues today.

THE HORATIO ALGER MYTH

IN THE nineteenth century, Horatio Alger wrote a series of novels with a similar theme: each story was about a young, impoverished boy who beat the odds and was able to rise above poverty through hard work and determination alone. These stories helped shape the "pull yourself up by the bootstraps" belief in the United States that anyone, regardless of wealth, has an equal shot at success if only they work hard enough.[19]

The Horatio Alger myth largely ignores privilege, systemic oppression, and prejudice. While in an ideal society everyone would start from an equal playing field, this simply isn't the case in the U.S. and in other nations. The myth suggests that perseverance and hard work alone lead to success, which leads to upward mobility in society. But if we look at identities through an intersectional lens, we see that wealth is only one aspect of someone's life. There are other factors we can't ignore. From dealing with housing and employment discrimination based on race to unequal access to education and a safe environment, not everyone has to overcome the same obstacles on their journey to succeed in society.

When we hold the belief that "anyone can succeed if they just set their mind to it," we also give credence to the flip side of that myth: that those who *don't* succeed aren't "trying hard enough." This places the blame solely on the individuals in need rather than on the systems of power supporting the barriers and disadvantages that oppress them, no matter how hard they work or try. The Horatio Alger myth also perpetuates negative stereotypes and generalizations, because those who believe it might view historically excluded and underrepresented groups of people that face systemic barriers as less worthy and even "lazy" if they don't have the same level of success as the dominant societal group. For example, when presented with data that Black Americans are paid less in comparison to white Americans, those who believe in the Horatio Alger myth might deduce that white Americans work harder. This type of belief can proliferate into stereotypes and generalizations about entire races and cultures of people.

I can see why it's tempting to buy into the Horatio Alger myth: we all want to pat ourselves on the back for our hard work and achievements. Believing in this myth allows individuals who benefit from privilege to ignore that the system is serving them—like a fish unaware of the water they're swimming in, ignoring that this water is toxic to others. It then becomes easy to turn away from societal injustices and fail to advocate for the equal treatment of others.

Acknowledging privilege is not equivalent to discrediting hard work and erasing someone's success. It just helps put things in perspective and highlight what needs to change in society so that everyone can have a fair shot. While free will certainly exists, there are accessibility concerns and barriers that exclude many with the will to succeed from equal access to opportunity. This is why many high-profile Black celebrities who have "made it" and grossed millions of dollars, like Oprah, LeBron James, and Colin Kaepernick, still acknowledge racial inequality and use their platforms to advocate for change. They know that these issues are bigger than their individual successes.

The main takeaway here is that a combination of our environments and our identities (both real and perceived) structure our life's possibilities. Let's take a look at two different scenarios.

Person A: Grows up in poverty in a household with a single parent working double shifts to pay the bills. This parent's highest level of education is a high school diploma, leaving A unsure as to how to navigate the college application process. A also has to get a job to help pay rent and isn't able to participate in after-school activities. A's neighborhood school receives significantly less funding than other schools, and crime is common within the student body, as A's fellow students try to achieve upward mobility through illegal activity.

Person B: Grows up in a stable and loving two-parent household, with parents who hold advanced degrees and expect their children to go to college. B is able to attend costly college prep courses and after-school activities. B's friends come from similar backgrounds, and they haven't been exposed to daily crime in their neighborhoods.

While both A and B have the chance to achieve their goals, get into a great school, find a high-paying job, and achieve upward mobility, it's significantly easier for Person B to do so. This person has fewer external or environmental factors that negatively impact the ability to focus energy and resources on education and personal development. Given this information, it is logical to conclude that Person A will have very different life possibilities than Person B, regardless of each's hard work and perseverance.

✹
DOES HAVING PRIVILEGE MAKE YOU A BAD PERSON?

ACKNOWLEDGING WHICH aspects of your life and identity may have led to advantages (or disadvantages) doesn't make you a "bad person." Recognizing privilege isn't meant to shame you, make you feel bad, or suggest that you've had an easy life. However, the process allows the veil of denial to be lifted in order to reveal a pathway toward more understanding, empathy, and equity.

Understanding privilege isn't cut-and-dried. Even as a Black woman, I'm able to look at my childhood and see areas in my life that helped me get where I am today. I grew up in a college-educated, two-parent household and was able to attend a top private school from fifth through twelfth grade. Even though I was one of few Black students, I still had the privilege of access to education and opportunity, which made college preparation and the application process easier for me. Being exposed to primarily white and wealthy spaces at a young age taught me how to "code switch" and blend into these types of spaces more effectively than a person of color who didn't share this access. I'm able to recognize my many advantages in life while also recognizing that being Black and a woman in a white and patriarchal society are not two of them.

Having privilege doesn't make you a bad person; it's what you do with it and how you acknowledge it that matters.

Q: How can ally communities help advocate for people + planet?

"First is just taking time to really, genuinely listen. Not to argue, not to debate peoples' lived experiences, not to share fragility or try to defend yourself for the privileges you hold. White supremacy is like a poison: you have to purge it before you can get towards a place of healing. That purging is never comfortable, but it must be done to move forward and understand the many injustices BIPOC face."

—Sabs Katz, low-impact vegan activist, cofounder of Intersectional Environmentalist

IE VOCAB: BIPOC, POC, QTBIPOC, QTPOC

BIPOC stands for Black, Indigenous, and people of color. **POC** stands for people of color. BIPOC was developed to ensure that Black and Indigenous people were not erased under the umbrella term "people of color." **QTBIPOC** and **QTPOC** stand for, respectively, queer and trans BIPOC and queer and trans POC. These terms are imperfect, and language shifts often occur in society. It's best to reference a specific racial or cultural group when you're speaking of them and to use these additional terms when referencing people of color as a collective group.

HOW DO PRIVILEGE AND ENVIRONMENTALISM INTERSECT?

THOSE WHO hold more power and privilege in society are less likely to be exposed to environmental injustice and hazards. No, the environment and climate don't discriminate, but people do, and therefore so do environmental policies.

Going back to the earlier statistic of lower funding in BIPOC schools versus primarily white schools, this funding gap also exists in community resources like parks, community gardens, and green spaces, meaning that access to these resources also varies along racial lines. Systemic housing discrimination practices like redlining—the refusal to insure mortgages in and near Black neighborhoods—have added to the climate burden by siloing communities of color in areas that are more likely to be plagued by environmental injustice. Black and Latinx people in the U.S. experience an "air pollution burden," in which they are exposed to 56 percent and 63 percent more pollution than is caused by their consumption, and which is linked to higher rates of cardiovascular and respiratory issues.[20] The opposite is true for white Americans, who experience a "pollution advantage," in which they breathe in 17 percent less air pollution than they cause.[21]

In addition to this housing discrimination and increased exposure to both air and water pollution, an EPA report from 2018 revealed that more than half of the nine million Americans living near hazardous waste sites are people of color.[22] Black Americans are "three times more likely to die from exposure to air pollutants than their white counterparts."[23]

One recent example of environmental injustice is the Flint, Michigan, water crisis. Back in April 2014, Flint officials, looking to cut costs, switched the city water supply from Lake Huron to the Flint River. This cost-saving measure left residents of Flint, one of the poorest cities in the U.S. with a majority Black population, with discolored, malodorous water and unimaginable health consequences that are still being felt to this day.[24]

In 2015, after assessing the water quality, the EPA and Virginia

Tech found that the water from the pipeline had dangerous levels of lead, a cause of serious health issues, especially in terms of child development. The lead collected in one Flint water sample was greater than one thousand parts per billion, which is nearly seventy times the EPA drinking water action level.[25] Not only was the water laced with lead, but it wasn't being treated with anything to prevent corrosion of the iron piping and leaching of additional lead into the water supply. It's very difficult to imagine this same scenario playing out in a wealthy, middle-class, or primarily white neighborhood. The local government was more willing to take an environmental gamble in a community with fewer resources to gather and use against the government. Sadly, it took years of media scrutiny to finally lead to a settlement for the Flint community, which had to survive off bottled water for years and whose children will be forever impacted by lead poisoning.

Another example of environmental injustice is the aftermath of Hurricane Katrina, which struck New Orleans in 2005. When discussing climate change and the increasing frequency of natural disasters, Georgiana Bostean, a professor of environmental science, health, and policy at Chapman University, confirms, "The impacts are not borne equally by all populations." The worst damage of the hurricane, Bostean writes, was found in "predominantly Black neighborhoods, yet the relief was far slower and inadequate compared with that provided in predominantly white and higher-income neighborhoods, despite those being less impacted."[26]

People of color and low-income communities suffer from a lack of systemic protection before, during, and after natural disasters.[27] Prior to a disaster, they are more likely to be underserved by relief agencies and have inadequate disaster insurance, and they are even more likely to live in unsafe and unprotected housing that hasn't been disaster-proofed.[28] During the disaster, due to language barriers or lack of access to communications, these residents might be unable to access warnings and safety instructions.[29] After the disaster, the recovery process is slower for these communities due to disproportionately less access to loans and government assistance and due to increased stigma and racial bias as they attempt to find new homes.[30] Communities of color are also located closer to toxic waste sites, agricultural pollution, and landfills that can easily spill into neighborhoods with increased flooding.[31]

Natural disasters and climate events expose deeply embedded societal disparities. *New York Times* columnist David Brooks explained perfectly in a 2005 op-ed: hurricanes "wash away the surface of society, the settled way things have been done. They expose the underlying power structures, the injustices, the patterns of corruption and unacknowledged inequalities."[32] When the literal storms and environmental tragedies are over, what's left are case studies of privilege and inequality at play.

When thinking of the future of the environment and a potential climate crisis, this statement is especially alarming because underrepresented groups will continue to bear the brunt of disasters if nothing changes. Racism and bias exist in several spheres, and it's imperative to find solutions that allow everyone to breathe clean air, drink clean water, protect their homes, and exist safely in this world.

Having a safe home and environment is a basic human need, but unfortunately, the ability to do so has become deeply intertwined with privilege. In addition to environmental injustice, living sustainably can be a matter of privilege. Single-use items are more expensive, and plastic is found at higher rates in communities of color. Living on a plant-based diet and eating regenerative and organically grown products is nearly impossible in a state of food apartheid, in which communities of color are more likely to be found. So when educating others about sustainability, make sure to think about intersectionality and privilege first. Refrain from shaming those who are faced with systemic barriers to living low-waste and sustainably.

IE VOCAB: FOOD JUSTICE, FOOD APARTHEID, AND FOOD SOVEREIGNTY

The following definitions are courtesy of Dara Cooper, a national organizer of the National Black Food and Justice Alliance (blackfoodjustice.org).

"FOOD JUSTICE: A process whereby communities most impacted and exploited by our current corporate-controlled, extractive agricultural system shift power to reshape, redefine, and provide Indigenous, community-based solutions to accessing and controlling food that are humanizing, fair, healthy, accessible, racially equitable, environmentally sound, and just. A framework going beyond access to ensure that our communities have not only the right but the ability to have community control of our food, including the means of production and distribution.

"FOOD APARTHEID: The systematic destruction of Black self-determination to control our food (including land, resource theft, and discrimination), a hypersaturation of destructive foods and predatory marketing, and a blatantly discriminatory corporate-controlled food system that results in our communities suffering from some of the highest rates of heart disease and diabetes of all time. Many tend to use the term 'food desert'; however, 'food apartheid' is a much more accurate representation of the structural racialized inequities perpetuated through our current system.

"FOOD SOVEREIGNTY: This entails a shift away from the corporate agricultural system and towards our own governance of our own food systems. It is about our right to healthy food produced through ecologically sound and sustainable methods, with the right to define and ultimately control our own food and agriculture systems. Shifting from an exclusively rights-based framework to one of governance puts the needs of those who work and consume at all points of the food chain at the center, rather than the demands of corporations and markets."[33] —Dara Cooper, the National Black Food and Justice Alliance

Q: Accessibility and disability aren't always discussed in the environmental movement or sustainability curriculums. What do you wish those who want to be allies knew about these topics and how they intersect with activism and environmentalism?

"It would be great if those who want to be allies to the disabled community could acknowledge the privileges and ableism that remains present in current environmentalism discussions. Eco-ableism creates a divide that 'others' disabled environmentalists—and considering the fact that at least 15 percent of the world's population lives with a disability, this is counterproductive to the idea of being an inclusive movement. Allies to the disabled environmentalist community should help advocate for accessible sustainable practices and materials that are considerate of disabled needs."

—Ambika Rajyagor, intersectional feminist and disabled rights advocate, cofounder of Disabled & Outdoors

Q: What piece of advice do you have for the next generation of LGBTQ+ environmentalists?

"Queerness exists in nature all around us. Nature never gives us binaries, either/ors, male or female, black or white, gay or straight. Instead, nature gives us queerness and fluidity, metamorphosis, change and magical infinite variety. So, my advice to the next generation of LGBTQ+ environmentalists is to first see your queerness as natural, then know that you are loved by this earth and utilize your unique lenses and queer identity as a special tool to create an even more intersectional and queer climate community."

—Wyn Wiley / Pattie Gonia, drag queen, intersectional environmentalist, photographer, creative director, and outdoorist

THE IE PLEDGE BREAKOUT AND DISCUSSION:

I will use my privilege to advocate for Black and Brown lives in spaces where this message is often silenced. I will amplify the messages of Black, Indigenous, and POC activists and environmental leaders.

HOW CAN WE USE PRIVILEGE TO CREATE CHANGE?

IGNORING THE existence of systemic inequality and privilege only leads to denial, which allows unjust systems to flourish. If we don't name the problem and really understand it, then we can't take action to right the wrongs of the past and move forward with a more equitable society and environment for all people regardless of race, culture, or background.

Many important decisions about the environments in which we live are disproportionately made by those with privilege and power. It is therefore imperative that we amplify the voices, efforts, and concerns of historically excluded groups that have been negatively impacted by social and environmental injustice. It's essential to dive into the systemic racism and discrimination that also exist within the environmental movement and to acknowledge how many environmental protections haven't been equally extended to BIPOC communities.

BIPOC and people from the LGBTQ+ and disabled communities don't get to ignore the absence of privilege in their lives, because it has real-world consequences that impact their well-being and safety. Ignoring the existence of privilege is a privilege in its own right.

If you'd like to strive toward being an ally and dismantling systems of oppression in the environmental movement, first understand your privileges and how your own identities intersect.

CHAPTER DISCUSSION QUESTIONS:

- **WHICH ASPECTS** of my identity, if any, felt most impactful in my upbringing? This can be race, religion or spirituality, gender, sexuality, socioeconomic status, geographic location, and other identity aspects.
- **WHICH ASPECTS** in the above question were less impactful in my upbringing and why? Are there any aspects that I haven't considered previously that may have influenced the way I perceive the world?
- **HOW DO** my overlapping identities intersect?
- **WHICH IDENTITY** aspects does the world around me use as identifiers before getting to know me?
- **WHICH IDENTITY** aspects would require a conversation in order for someone else to learn about me?
- **ARE THERE** parts of my identity that I'd like to explore more? If so, how can I begin that journey?

Next, remember that allyship can be a verb, not just a noun. It's a journey of listening, learning, taking feedback, and allowing others to lead the way.

QUESTIONS:

-  **HOW CAN** I practice active, nonjudgmental, nondefensive, and engaged listening when learning about different communities outside my own?
- **IF SOMEONE** acknowledges that my actions have harmed them, intentionally or not, how can I self-reflect and assess in order to approach future conversations differently?
- **WHAT RESOURCES** can I utilize to learn more about questions I have regarding another cultural community before asking someone from that community?

Lastly, oftentimes communities may have already come up with solutions to issues pertaining to how to reach social and environmental justice, but they might be in need of affiliation, validation, and support. Here are questions to ask yourself to aid in that support and avoid saviorism or repeating work others have already done.

QUESTIONS:

- **HOW CAN I IDENTIFY** grassroots efforts that have already occurred and research injustices pertaining to communities outside my own?
- **HOW CAN I AMPLIFY** the work that's already being done and use my personal strengths to aid the cause?
- **HOW CAN I CREATE** space in my school, organization, workplace, or community for voices that have been marginalized?

✳ **EVEN IF** my peers, coworkers, or community members aren't aware of systemic oppression, how can I begin to raise awareness with them and start conversations in spaces used by people who might not be aware?

Q: How can ally communities use their privilege to advocate for people + planet?

"Stand up to those in power when it is necessary, shut up when it's time to listen to those most affected by systems of oppression, and speak up when your white peers are harming others with their ignorance. Without dismantling white supremacy and achieving environmental justice for all people, we cannot reverse climate change and build a regenerative future."

—Phil Aiken, environmental creative, cofounder of Intersectional Environmentalist

CHAPTER 4

Who's Affected: The Reality for BIPOC Communities

IN THIS chapter, we'll explore research and data that paints a full picture of the devastating impacts of environmental injustice and its close ties to racial identity. The environmental justice crisis has been ongoing for decades, and it has deleteriously impacted the health, safety, and well-being of people of color globally.

A note on data collection: In this chapter, much of the data covered references and relies on the U.S. census, which has historic flaws and inaccuracies. Presently, this data is the most accurate way to assess racial demographics and how they've shifted over time; these figures help highlight environmental injustice and how it affects the U.S. population with disproportionate impacts. The majority of the data referenced in this first section is from the American Public

Health Association report "Climate Change, Health, and Equity: A Guide for Local Health Departments," which examines the intersections of climate change, public health, and equity. I strongly recommend reading the full report to explore even further.[1]

✸

BLACK AMERICANS AND CLIMATE INJUSTICE

AS OF 2016, African Americans make up 13.3 percent (forty-two million people) of the total U.S. population, or 14.5 percent (forty-six million people) when you include those who are multiracial.[2] The places with the highest relative Black populations are Mississippi, Georgia, Louisiana, Maryland, and the nation's capital, Washington, DC.[3] The U.S. census predicts that the Black population will increase to 15 percent of the total population by 2060.[4]

To better understand the environmental outcomes for Black communities in the U.S., it's important to look at both historical and social determinants of these outcomes. To start, we can turn to the U.S. slave trade, from approximately 1526 to 1867, in which around 388,000 people were kidnapped from Africa, forced into slavery, and exploited to work as unpaid servants and cotton, tobacco, and other agricultural laborers in the U.S. The brutal conditions of slavery and the disregard for Black life were precursors for the discriminatory ideals, policies, and practices that led to the systematic disenfranchisement of Black citizens in America.[5,6]

The Jim Crow laws that followed slavery in the late 1800s to mid-1900s upheld ideas of racial hierarchy in U.S. society. Jim Crow laws mandated the segregation of schools, restrooms, public transportation, parks and recreational areas, restaurants, and more.[7] These different facilities for the Black population were not "separate but equal," as government officials dictated they should be. In actuality, the Black facilities were almost always inferior to those granted to white U.S. citizens, and the Black population was routinely denied the right to even participate in elections despite having the legal right to vote.[8]

Redlining, the practice of banks and mortgage lenders denying Black citizens loans for homes in well-maintained neighborhoods, is a major factor in where Black citizens have been allowed to live.[9] The term "redlining" is defined by the Federal Reserve as the "presumed practice of mortgage lenders of drawing red lines around portions of a map to indicate areas or neighborhoods in which they do not want to make loans."[10] Redlining completely flouts the Fair Housing Act of 1968, which is supposed to stop discrimination against borrowers, buyers, or renters based on religion, sex, origin, disability, and race.[11] Unfortunately, systemic racism still exists in present-day mortgage-lending policies.

Slavery, Jim Crow laws, and redlining are three historical practices that led to deep-seated societal attitudes toward the Black community and are key determinants of the specific locations of Black communities in the U.S. and their proximity to environmental hazards. These historical practices have led to present-day social, health, and environmental inequality.

In a 2009 USC study, "The Climate Gap: Inequalities in How Climate Change Hurts Americans and How to Close the Gap," researchers found that "African Americans on average emit nearly 20 percent less greenhouse gases than non-Hispanic whites per capita. Though **less responsible** for climate change, African Americans are **significantly more vulnerable** to its effects than non-Hispanic whites." This is a recurring theme we'll see throughout this chapter: those who are **least** responsible for the climate crisis are often the **most** impacted and burdened by it.

✦ SOME OF THOSE VULNERABILITIES INCLUDE: ✦

AIR QUALITY:

IN THEIR 2008 study, "A Climate of Change: African Americans, Global Warming, and a Just Climate Policy for the U.S.," J. Andrew Hoerner and Nia Robinson found:

- ☀ **71 PERCENT** of African Americans live in counties that are in violation of federal air pollution standards.[12]
- ☀ **78 PERCENT** of African Americans live within thirty miles of a coal-fired power plant.[13]
- ☀ **AFRICAN AMERICANS** have 36 percent higher rates of asthma than whites, an affliction closely associated with the presence of air pollution.[14]
- ☀ **ASTHMA** is three times as likely to lead to emergency room visits or death for African Americans.[15]

EXTREME HEAT:

- ☀ **43 PERCENT** of African Americans live in urban "heat islands," neighborhoods with fewer green spaces, diminished tree cover, and increased asphalt and concrete, which retain heat and lead to higher ambient temperatures.[16]
- ☀ **AS A RESULT,** temperatures in historically redlined neighborhoods are up to 12.6 degrees hotter than non-redlined neighborhoods, creating "heat islands" in Black neighborhoods.[17]
- ☀ **THE CLIMATE** crisis is expected to increase both the frequency and intensity of extreme heat events, and African Americans suffer heat-related deaths at a higher rate than white communities.[18]

☀ **EXTREME HEAT** increases ozone levels, which further exacerbates respiratory and cardiovascular disease.[19]

LATINX AMERICANS AND CLIMATE INJUSTICE

AS OF 2016, the Hispanic population (of any race) accounts for 17.8 percent of the total U.S. population and is projected by the U.S. Census Bureau to grow to 27.5 percent by the year 2060.[20] The U.S. census defines "Hispanic" as "a person of Cuban, Mexican, Puerto Rican, South or Central American, or other Spanish culture or origin regardless of race."[21] It's important to note that many people who are considered Hispanic by the U.S. census don't identify as such and may prefer other terminology based on nationality, history, politics, language, and more, such as Chicano/a/x, Tejano, Mexican(a/o), Xicano, or Latino/e/x. In this chapter, I will use the term "Latinx" (a gender-neutral alternative to Latino, Latina, or Latine—the latter of which is also gender-neutral).

The Latinx population in the U.S. is the largest ethnic minority group. According to the census, as of 2016 there are 56 million Latinx people in the U.S.; this number will likely almost double by 2060.[22] The majority of Latinx people in the current U.S. population are second- or third-generation (meaning their parents or grandparents immigrated to the U.S.).[23] As of 2019, the largest Latinx populations are in states that border Mexico: California, Texas, Arizona, and New Mexico, with Texas and California accounting for 45 percent of the total Latinx population.[24] Latinx populations are also growing in other states, with more than twelve states having Latinx populations of over one million in 2019.[25]

Environmental injustice also disproportionately impacts Latinx communities in the U.S., and it's important to examine the historic and social determinants that have caused these environmental outcomes. We can point to systemic discrimination in immigration, health care, education, employment, and beyond to find the roots of environmental injustice pertaining to the Latinx community.

Latinx people have lived in what is now the United States since the sixteenth century, with over one hundred thousand Spanish-speaking residents becoming U.S. citizens in the 1800s, when Florida, Louisiana, and part of Mexico were annexed (or added/colonized) by the U.S. During the gold rush and the Mexican-American War,[26] the U.S. brutally invaded Mexico, instigated by U.S. president James K. Polk and other government officials dedicated to Manifest Destiny—a cultural belief that Americans were entitled to expand westward and take any land they found as their own, despite all the Indigenous people who already lived there and the cultures they would violently disrupt.[27] This belief had long-lasting impacts on both Indigenous and Latinx peoples, through social stigmas and policies. The Treaty of Guadalupe Hidalgo ended the Mexican-American War, and California, Arizona, New Mexico, Colorado, and Utah became part of the U.S. This sparked a smaller but notable migration of Mexicans and Chileans to California. The impacts of the war were long-lasting, leading to distrust between the United States and Mexico and hostility toward Latinx people.

Following migrations after the gold rush, Latinx immigrants were met with racism and discrimination, which only intensified with increased Latinx immigration in the 1900s.[28] As the American economy expanded with new jobs in infrastructure and agriculture and as political turmoil and revolution occurred in Mexico, there was a great migration of Mexican immigrants to the U.S. in the twentieth century.[29] The Latinx population expanded even further during the Second World War, with the high demand for both agricultural and defense-related jobs. This influx, along with those fleeing the Castro revolution in Cuba, brought the Latinx population in the U.S. into the millions, and that population developed and solidified into intergenerational communities within the U.S.[30]

Even though the Latinx community has contributed greatly to the American economy and to the growth of its infrastructure, education, and culture, it's still faced with stressors, discrimination, racism, and poor environmental quality and working conditions. In 2014, 26.5 percent of the Latinx population didn't have health insurance, and in 2015, one in five Latinx families reported living in poverty.[31] Startlingly, more than 60 percent of Latinx communities in the U.S. are in areas impacted by air pollution, flooding, and extreme heat.[32]

✦ ENVIRONMENTAL INJUSTICES IMPACTING THE ✦ LATINX COMMUNITY INCLUDE:

EXTREME HEAT:

✳ **LATINX PEOPLE** are 21 percent more likely to live in a heat island than white Americans, and over 4.3 million Latinx families live in a home without access to air-conditioning.[33]

✳ **LATINX PEOPLE** account for almost half of the U.S. farmworker population and 92 percent of the farmworker population in California, and they are three times as likely to die from a heat-related death on the job as white Americans.[34]

AIR QUALITY, FOOD SECURITY, AND AGRICULTURE:

✳ **NEARLY 50 PERCENT** of Latinx individuals live in counties that frequently violate clean air and ozone standards.[35]

✳ **OVER 1.8 MILLION** Latinx people live within a half-mile radius of oil and gas development (plants and facilities).[36]

✳ **A 2019 STUDY** found that Latinx Californians are exposed to 39 percent higher levels of air pollution than white Californians.[37]

✳ **21 PERCENT** of Latinx individuals are food insecure, which the U.S. Department of Agriculture defines as those with a "lack of consistent access to enough food for an active, healthy life."[38]

☀ **THE LATINX** community accounts for 70 percent of the combined population of the ten zip codes with the highest pesticide use in California.[39]

INDIGENOUS COMMUNITIES AND CLIMATE INJUSTICE (USA)

THE 2010 U.S. census, which I'd like to note again has had a long history of discriminatory practices, listed 5.2 million self-identifying Native Americans and Native Alaskans, which includes people with two Indigenous parents, multiracial Indigenous peoples, and self-identifying Native Americans.[40] While the U.S. census refers to the Indigenous people of North America as Native Americans/Indians and Native Alaskans in their data collection, it's important to note that while the term "Native American" has been widely used in the twentieth century, there are differing opinions within the Indigenous community on appropriate terminology. Out of respect, whenever possible it's best to research and pinpoint the specific tribes being referenced. If you'd like to learn more about the Native land you're currently on and the history of its people, visit Native-Land.ca.

In this chapter, I will be using the term "Indigenous" when referring to the people who are Indigenous to the land that is now known as the United States. Since 2000, the Indigenous population has increased by 27 percent, with the vast majority of its people living on or near reservations.[41] The highest proportions are concentrated in Alaska, Oklahoma, and New Mexico and the highest populations in California, Oklahoma, and Arizona.[42] Before we dive further, I want to remind you that intersectionality must include Indigenous peoples, who are often erased even from conversations on diversity, equity, and inclusion. We must hold space for them and honor their histories, perspectives, and knowledge.

The genocide and inhumane treatment of Indigenous peoples and theft of their land, homes, and ecosystems is a shameful legacy of American colonization. Disease, violence, forced relocations, destructions of cultural practices, and other factors contributed to the collapse and genocide of Indigenous people starting after 1492, when Christopher Columbus set foot in the Americas.

While it is difficult to find a precise estimate for the number of lives lost and so brutally taken, following Columbus's arrival, nearly fifty-five million Indigenous people were killed by either violence or disease (including smallpox, measles, and influenza).[43] In 2010, Indigenous people made up 1.7 percent of the U.S. population, but they are expected to grow to 2.4 percent by 2060 and to continue rising.[44] When compared with other races in the U.S., Indigenous peoples have a lower than average life expectancy by 5.5 years, which can be attributed to chronic illness, liver disease, mellitus, and suicide.[45] In the present, the painful legacy of conquest and colonialism contributes greatly to the environmental and social injustices that Indigenous communities face. It's important to also note that data collection, even for environmental justice studies, has often left out Indigenous peoples. More thorough studies are needed to truly present the totality of environmental injustices faced by Indigenous people.

✦ ENVIRONMENTAL INJUSTICES IMPACTING THE ✦ INDIGENOUS COMMUNITY INCLUDE:

AIR QUALITY:

☀ **12 PERCENT** of people living in tribal communities are impacted by asthma. This is almost **double the national average.** This increase has been linked to poor indoor air quality.[46]

FOOD SCARCITY:

☀ **SEVERAL INDIGENOUS** communities are living in a state of food apartheid, with a lack of access to food and higher costs of healthy and nutritious foods.[47]

WATER ACCESS:

☀ **INDIGENOUS PEOPLE** in the U.S. are **the least likely** to have access to **safe running water.** With a lack of access to clean water for cooking, cleaning, and handwashing during the COVID-19 pandemic, the Navajo Nation was hit with an infection rate of 2,500 per hundred thousand residents— surpassing that of the nation's epicenter at the time, New York City in early 2020.[48]

☀ **20 PERCENT** of rural Alaskan homes **lack access to piped water** and a flushable toilet, which can leave these populations without access to potable water and clean water to use for washing.[49]

☀ **FIFTY-EIGHT OUT OF** every one thousand Native American households **lack plumbing,** compared with three out of every one thousand white households.[50]

☀ **ONGOING PIPELINE** projects threaten the **health of primary waterways for drinking water** to Indigenous communities and would increase exposure to contaminants.

DISPLACEMENT:

☀ **INDIGENOUS PEOPLE** have been continuously displaced by U.S. government–mandated land use projects.

Q: What's something you'd like the environmental community to consider more and prioritize in their climate agendas?

"When we commit acts of violence against the earth from extractive methods through a capitalistic lens, we continue to perpetuate these traumas and acts of violence for dominance, for profit, and for control—where it deems the lives of those near those dirty infrastructure projects as expendable. And what we don't hear enough are the stories of violence, homicide, and rescue missions of Indigenous women and girls (and peoples) fleeing the man camps near those pipelines or projects, the high rates of domestic violence, sexual assault, homicides/assassinations, and human/sex/drug trafficking. The protection of the people needs to be prioritized in all climate agendas."

—Jordan Marie Daniel, founder of Rising Hearts

AAPI (ASIAN AMERICANS AND NATIVE HAWAIIANS/PACIFIC ISLANDERS) AND CLIMATE INJUSTICE

AS OF 2019, the Asian population in the U.S. is around 7 percent of the total population and almost doubled to 23.2 million people within a two-decade time span.[51] The U.S. census classifies a member of the Asian racial group as "a person having origins in any of the original peoples of the Far East, Southeast Asia, or the Indian subcontinent including Cambodia, China, India, Japan, Korea, Malaysia, Pakistan, the Philippine Islands, Thailand, and Vietnam."[52] The Asian American population is projected to increase from 5.9 percent to 9.1 percent in 2060.[53]

The Native Hawaiian and Pacific Islander population was one of the fastest-growing racial groups between 2000 and 2010.[54] The census classifies the Native Hawaiian and Pacific Islander group as people from "Hawaii, Guam, Samoa, or other Pacific Islands." The 2020 census was the first year that the "Native Hawaiian and other Pacific Islander" population was classified separately from the "Asian population" option.[55] According to the 2019 U.S. Census Bureau estimates, this group represents about 0.4 percent of the total U.S. population (about 1.4 million people).[56] The largest population concentrations are located in Hawaii, California, Washington, and Texas.[57]

It's important to note that the term "AAPI" encompasses a very wide range of identities, nationalities, and cultures, which means that experiences, histories, and social/environmental outcomes will vary greatly. While AAPI is one of the fastest-growing racial demographics in the U.S., there is, unfortunately, a lack of data pertaining to the historic intersections of health, social justice, and environment;

some aggregated data also distorts statistics for Native Hawaiians and Pacific Islanders. This lack in data and representation highlights a problematic history of Asian, Native Hawaiian, and Pacific Islander erasure that should be addressed within the intersectional environmental movement. Next I'll give a brief overview of only a few historic and social determinants that have led to negative social, health, and environmental outcomes for the AAPI community.

The COVID-19 pandemic shone an ugly light on the pervasiveness of anti-Asian racism, which has roots far beyond the virus originating in Wuhan. During the California gold rush (1848 to 1855) and right before the construction of the transcontinental railroad, many Chinese laborers immigrated to the western U.S. in the hope of finding work.[58] Xenophobia, the prejudice against or dislike of immigrants, and competition fears arose in California, which resulted in a new law, one of the first anti-Asian pieces of legislation, that taxed Chinese miners.

A few decades later, in 1893, Americans staged a coup, overthrowing and occupying the Kingdom of Hawaii after Queen Lili'uokalani assumed the throne.[59] This occupation led to annexation and an aggressive push from American settlers to ban the teaching of Native Hawaiian language and culture, in addition to destroying Indigenous government structures and policies (including universal health care).[60] The Hawaiian language prohibition wasn't lifted until 1986, and revitalization efforts to infuse Hawaiian history into school curriculums are ongoing.

In 1941, after the attack on Pearl Harbor by the Japanese government, an increase in anti-Asian discrimination led to human rights violations.[61] Under an executive order by then president Franklin Roosevelt, many people of Japanese descent were forced to live separately from society in internment camps from 1942 to 1945.[62] The isolation from society and discrimination had traumatic and negative health impacts, both mental and physical, on Japanese

Americans. Compounding the prejudice fostered by the internment camps and by repeated aggressive attempts to prevent Asian immigration, the Vietnam and Korean wars increased anti-Asian discrimination that has carried on within the U.S. to the present day.

✦ ENVIRONMENTAL INJUSTICES IMPACTING ✦ THE AAPI COMMUNITY INCLUDE:

- ❋ **WHEN COMPARED** with other racial groups in the U.S., **Chinese and Korean Americans** have the **highest mean cancer risk** from air pollution exposure.[63]
- ❋ **SOUTHEAST AND** **South Asian** communities in the U.S. have the **fourth and fifth** highest risk of cancer stemming from air pollution.[64]
- ❋ **50 PERCENT** of Asian American communities lack access to **tree cover and green spaces** that can provide shade.[65]
- ❋ **32 PERCENT** of Asian Americans live in communities where **heat-retaining surfaces** cover over half of the ground.[66]
- ❋ **BY 2100,** Hawaii is projected to experience a sea level rise that's **about 1 to 2.5 feet higher** than global averages.[67]
- ❋ **84 PERCENT** of Native Hawaiian and Pacific Islander neighborhoods in Los Angeles, California, are located within one mile of a Superfund site—an area with high concentrations of hazardous material contamination. This is the **highest of any racial demographic.**[68]

Q: How is the #StopAsianHate movement directly tied to our fight against the systems of oppression that also hurt the environment?

"The #StopAsianHate movement is directly tied to our fight against the systems of oppression that hurt the environment because they are the *same* systems: vulnerable communities are all oppressed by the institutions of white supremacy, white nationalism, and capitalism.

"When the most vulnerable Asians are being attacked—elders and those least assimilated—the institution of white supremacy wins. The same institution that has gerrymandered white and Black neighborhoods for generations, the same institution that continues to finance and fund fossil fuels, the same institution that values profit over people and planet. Our fight is everyone's fight."

—Sophia Li, journalist, director, and climate activist

GLOBAL EXAMPLES

THE IMPACTS of colonialism are far-reaching, and environmental racism and injustice crises are occurring globally and growing at alarming rates. While the environmental justice movement as we know it started in the U.S. in the 1980s, environmental injustice holds no geographic boundaries. Climate activists in the Global South are not receiving the same support and recognition as climate activists and organizations in the Global North, even though southern climate issues are just as urgent and need global support.

Q: Why is it important for the media and climate community to focus not just on the Global North but on countries like Uganda?

"We are on the front lines of the climate crisis but we are not on the front pages of the world's newspapers. If the media and the climate community do not tell our stories, then we will not be able to get the justice that we deserve. Every activist has a story to tell, every story has a solution to give, and every solution has a life to change. Climate justice is only justice if it includes all of us. Erasing the voices of African and Black activists means erasing our stories, erasing our experiences, erasing the challenges that we are going through. We are the least responsible for the climate crisis but we are definitely among the most affected by climate change. Climate justice is racial justice. Environmental justice starts with listening to the most affected people and communities."

—Vanessa Nakate, climate justice activist and founder of the Rise Up movement, Uganda

INTERNATIONAL WASTE DISPOSAL

ONE EXAMPLE of environmental injustice that transcends borders is the disposal of numerous types of waste from the Global North to the Global South.

The global waste trade dates back decades and has been investigated by international organizations since the 1980s. Overconsumption of new technology and the societal shift to replace and update technology at rapid rates in the Global North have led to enormous amounts of waste being transported and discarded in the Global South. This literal trashing has exposed people in the Global South to environmental hazards that pollute the soil, air, and waterways with toxic waste and plastics.[69] While global legislation has helped tighten the restrictions on e-waste dumping, this disposal will likely only increase as technological innovation proliferates and the world becomes more virtual.

In 2013, the United Nations claimed that China had become the "largest e-waste dumping site in the world," with around 70 percent of electronic waste globally ending up in that country.[70] Everything from cell phones to air-conditioning units ended up in China, specifically in Guiyu, a southeastern town located in the country's manufacturing zone. A majority of the e-waste comes to China illegally: although the United Nations has set restrictions, the dumping practice continues at alarming rates as countries like the United States keep leaving their waste in the Global South.

And it's not just the dumping that presents a health threat. Once the waste reaches towns like Guiyu, laborers will try to break apart the electronics to find anything of value that has the potential to be resold. The streets are flooded with mounds of abandoned circuit boards, plastic, and wires, which leads to toxic pollution as the materials are burned or doused in acid. Toxic metals and hydrocarbon ashes are then released into the environment and onto workers themselves![71] Children in Guiyu have higher than average lead levels in their blood, which can stunt brain development, according to a study at Shantou University Medical College.[72]

Q: The Western climate movement often leaves out voices from countries that are most impacted and vulnerable in terms of the climate crisis. What do you wish more people knew about the climate challenges that the Philippines faces?

"Climate impacts in the Philippines are not just headlines about the last drought or the last typhoon. The climate story here is not just about disasters. We have environmentalists going up against fossil fuel companies who are silenced, threatened, and murdered; women and LGBTQ+ people attacked and violated in the aftermath of disasters in evacuation centers; communities complaining of health problems due to coal projects; climate justice activists being red-tagged by a government that doesn't bat an eyelash at human rights violations; and Indigenous groups robbed of land by corporations. We're facing injustices here day in and day out, wrought and exacerbated by climate change and its impacts in every imaginable way, from economics to human rights. But we also hold solutions and a great narrative of resistance: our people ousted a dictator, our women went up against major polluters, our youth are tirelessly calling out leaders for their inaction. I am of the opinion that the next generation will not take all the injustices of late sitting down. Our story continues."

—Beatrice Tulagan, climate organizer, the Philippines

SEA LEVEL RISE AND ISLAND NATIONS

SEA LEVEL rise is referenced frequently as an outcome of the climate crisis. As temperatures warm in some parts of the world, massive ice sheets and glaciers melt and enter the earth's oceans. The addition of these ice sheets and glaciers, along with the increased volume of warmed water (thermal expansion), lead to sea level rise.[73] When sea levels rise, people will be displaced—likely those least responsible for the climate crisis. Nations like Tuvalu, Kiribati, and the Marshall Islands are already dealing with salt water contaminating sources of drinking water and agricultural fields as a direct result of sea level rise.[74] If these peoples are forced to leave a no longer habitable island nation, who is responsible for providing refuge? This is an urgent question that needs to be answered to forestall a potential loss of land and culture as well as an impending refugee crisis.

Q: What do you wish more people understood about the impacts of colonialism in Africa or the unique climate challenges that the African continent faces?

"So many African countries are grappling with the remains of colonization and how it manifests today and continues to impact their economies, politics, resources, and land. This is not to say that African countries don't have their own challenges, but it is important to highlight that a majority of the political, economic, and cultural challenges they face today have been fueled by colonialism. In fact, in many ways, colonialism still exists within the continent; it's just not as overt as it was a hundred years ago. The extraction of resources, land, and labor of Africa today, influenced by capitalism, extends beyond economic, social, or political impact; it has major environmental consequences. Western countries and various global corporations continue to exploit many African countries by transferring waste, pollution, and environmental degradation to the continent. Every African country is different, with its own unique climate challenges, but ultimately, these environmental impacts will have and already have disproportionate health, economic, and environmental impacts throughout the continent, especially for low-income and rural communities.

"An overlapping theme internationally is that the world's largest contributors to the climate crisis are not bearing the brunt of climate injustice. The Global North should bear some, if not all, responsibility for the impending displacement of people and the increased extreme climate events that are a direct result of their industrialization and emissions. When power structures burden the Global South and communities of color in the U.S. with the responsibility to live through environmental injustice, and when these power structures abandon them without providing tools, resources, and solutions, it's a direct act of environmental racism."

—Abigail Abhaer Adekunbi Thomas, environmentalist and environmental advocate

THE IE PLEDGE BREAKOUT AND DISCUSSION:

I will proactively do the work to learn about environmental and social injustices that Black, Indigenous, and POC communities face without minimizing them. I will respect the boundaries of Black, Indigenous, and POC friends and activists, and not demand that they perform emotional labor or do the work for me.

This aspect of the pledge focuses heavily on proactively doing the work to learn about the specific environmental injustices facing BIPOC communities, without minimizing or excusing the clear instances of environmental racism. For far too long, environmental justice has been treated as an optional "add-on" to traditional environmental education, which does not help combat or stop environmental racism.

It's also important to be aware of lateral violence within social and environmental justice spaces, which occurs within marginalized groups (cultural and ethnic minorities, the LGBTQ+ community, low-income communities, religious groups, et cetera) when they are pitted against one another. Lateral violence encourages a cyclical and competitive comparison of the realities of different underrepresented communities and doesn't encourage empathy, compassion, or cross-cultural dialogue. We can hold space for different experiences without comparing experiences, especially of marginalized groups, and address the overarching systems of oppression impacting each community. Finding the common thread will encourage unification versus competition.

CHAPTER DISCUSSION QUESTIONS:

- **WHY HAVE** the demographics that have contributed the least to the climate crisis been hit the hardest by climate burdens?
- **HOW CAN** racial progress and equality also aid in environmental justice?
- **WHY HAVE** nations in the Global North chosen low-income cities in the Global South for their waste disposal? Does the potential for some economic benefit through the resale of waste outweigh the environmental and health hazards to these communities?
- **WHAT ARE** other global examples of environmental racism?
- **HOW CAN** I proactively research instances of environmental racism without burdening BIPOC to do the emotional labor for me?

CHAPTER 5

People + Planet

"Nuance allows a space for conversation, debate, and reflection on how sustainability has been taught, marketed, and implemented in our society today. Everyone comes to this space from a different set of upbringings, values, and needs—and that means people should be allowed to critique, challenge, and improve the pathway toward a more sustainable future. This will create the conditions for a more just and inclusive transition overall."

—Kristy Drutman, environmental media host and founder of
Brown Girl Green

AS HUMANS, we are all a part of a global ecosystem, and even the tiniest of our actions, like what we eat or buy, have a ripple effect on the world around us. Sometimes choices are driven by our values or upbringing; other times they're rooted in survival, and alternatives aren't available. Within this chapter, we'll discuss fashion, renewable energy, and veganism—topics pertinent to the current cultural zeitgeist—and we'll reexamine them through the lens of intersectional environmentalism now that you understand IE. We'll leave room for nuance and spend extra time exploring perspectives that aren't always elevated in the mainstream environmental narrative but should be. I hope this demonstrates a few examples of how intersectional environmentalist thinking can be applied to almost any topic and is worth considering to ensure that all voices have a seat at the table and both people and planet are advocated for.

FASHION

WHAT WE wear has an impact on both people and the planet. The fashion industry is one of the most polluting industries in the world, producing 10 percent of global carbon emissions.[1] "Fast fashion," a term coined in the *New York Times* in the 1980s, describes a shift in the fashion industry to speed up manufacturing and shipping to keep up with consumer demand[2]—a demand that was carefully cultivated by fashion brands to change consumer behavior and make people want more and more, and quickly. Fast fashion is largely responsible for the shockingly high emissions, waste, and harm caused by the apparel industry.

Prior to the 1990s, shopping for clothing in the United States was based more on need. Clothing was also more durably made and was intended to last. Fashion insiders had the privilege of previewing collections during runway shows and private exhibitions before trends hit the shelves, but for the average American, clothing was mostly purchased on an as-needed basis. With the increased availability of clothing and the explosion of cable TV in the 1980s and '90s, consumer trends started to shift. With networks like MTV showcasing the latest trends, shoppers began to dive further into their personal styles than ever before and chase the instant gratification that came with buying new things.

It's unfortunate but simple: if the styles and trends keep changing, consumers will just keep buying and buying to stay on trend—especially when the price of clothing becomes more affordable.

Pre–fast fashion culture, stores wouldn't restock their inventory every other week with new styles. Consumers had no reason to return to the same store over and over again because they'd just be staring at the same clothes they saw the week before. To increase sales, fast fashion giants like Zara and H&M started to regularly rotate in new items at cheaper prices so consumers would always have something new to buy.[3] Instead of taking months to develop new designs, fast fashion brands were able to minimize the production-to-store pipeline to just a few weeks! Suddenly a new fashion industry emerged, one that was driven less by need and quality than by how quickly it could reach consumers. This disregard for quality has led to clothing waste in our landfills. Constantly changing trends have encouraged consumers to discard clothing that's no longer "in style" even if it's still wearable.

Fast fashion doesn't only revolve around vanity or the desire to be stylish; the fast fashion industry has actually altered the way our brains experience pleasure and has made shopping an addiction.[4] In 2007, a team of researchers at Stanford and Carnegie Mellon used fMRI technology to examine the brains of test subjects as they bought clothing, and here's what they found:

* ✸ **WHEN SHOPPING** for a preferred item—something the subject really wanted—the brain's pleasure center, the nucleus accumbens, increased in activity.
* ✸ **WHEN PRESENTED** with an excessively priced/expensive item, the insula, which processes pain, showed activity.
* ✸ **TO SUMMARIZE:** When we shop, distinct circuits in the brain are activated based on how much we want an item and how we process the cost of the item. If the cost is excessive, we then have to grapple with the brain's pleasure center and perform a cost-benefit analysis of what might bring us pleasure and the financial impact of the cost.[5]

By contrast, when we think about fast fashion, which has lower-priced goods, the cost-benefit analysis our brains perform is more straightforward. The item is something we want, which brings us pleasure, and it's on sale and affordable, which also brings us pleasure.[6] This means of instant gratification from the fast fashion complex is a recipe for disaster for our brains, our wallets, supply chains, and the planet. Just when you think it won't get any worse, social media influencer culture has encouraged direct-to-consumer and online retail fast fashion brands to sell even more—and they don't even need a storefront.

Now that we have an understanding of what fast fashion is and how this system encourages us to constantly consume, let's examine how rapid consumption of apparel impacts people and the planet. As mentioned earlier, the fashion industry is one of the most environmentally damaging industries for a variety of different reasons. Here are some statistics:

* ✸ **AS OF** 2015, the world consumes 400 percent more clothing than it did twenty years ago, producing around eighty billion pieces of new clothing every year.[7]

- ✳ **AMERICANS THROW** away thirteen million tons of textiles each year.[8]
- ✳ **WASHING CLOTHES** releases microplastics into our waterways and ecosystems, the equivalent of fifty billion plastic water bottles each year.[9]
- ✳ **TEXTILE EMISSIONS** are expected to increase by 60 percent if things do not change.[10]
- ✳ **THE FASHION** industry is the world's second-largest industrial consumer of water. It takes seven hundred gallons to produce one cotton shirt and two thousand to produce one pair of jeans.[11]
- ✳ **IT REQUIRES** extensive amounts of energy to create textiles from plastic, which also releases petroleum and volatile particulate matter into the atmosphere.[12]

✦ THE FASHION INDUSTRY HAS ALSO CONTRIBUTED ✦ TO HUMAN RIGHTS AND CIVIL RIGHTS VIOLATIONS:

- ✳ **THE U.S.** Department of Labor and other investigative agencies have repeatedly found evidence of forced child labor and slavery within the fashion industry.[13]
- ✳ **IN 2013,** over 2,500 garment workers were injured and over a hundred were killed in the collapse of an unsafe eight-floor garment factory building in Dhaka, Bangladesh.[14]

In addition to enduring unsafe working conditions, female garment workers are left especially vulnerable to harassment. According to the Global Fund for Women, approximately 75 percent of garment workers globally are women; the total garment worker population includes tens of millions of people.[15] With no global standard for the treatment of garment workers, many must work long hours for low pay and are vulnerable to harassment and abuse at work.

- ☀ **68 PERCENT** of female garment workers in Cambodia reported feeling uncomfortable and unsafe at work.
- ☀ **60 PERCENT** of female garment workers in Bangladesh have experienced intimidation or threats while at work.
- ☀ **34 PERCENT** of female garment workers in Vietnam have said they'd experienced harassment while in the workplace.

Global legislation needs to extend to protect garment workers as well as the planet. While many garment facilities may be concentrated in the Global South, the swelling of this industry can largely be attributed to consumption in the Global North. Corporations looking to lower production costs have created an industry that cuts corners by exploiting people and the earth by using child labor, shirking safety standards, paying substandard wages, and prioritizing profit over planet.

Q: How can we start building a diverse and ethical fashion industry that doesn't exploit garment workers and the environment?

"I think the project of fast fashion was rooted in building a sense of apathy in the consumer, whether it's where their clothes come from, who made them, or where clothes will go at the end of their life cycle.

"For me, sustainable fashion means constantly asking questions, interrogating why the fashion system operates in the way that it does.

"By definition, the word 'sustainable' means to maintain something at a certain rate or level. However, the modern fashion system functions in a largely colonial manner, predicated on the exploitation of resources and labor. This is why sustainable fashion is so important—we're reorienting our relationship not only with fashion, but with land, labor, and art.

"In order to build an intersectional future for ethical fashion—one that doesn't exploit garment workers and the environment—I think it's helpful to begin by thinking of fashion as a product of land and labor, and reorienting our relationship to both of those things.

"When we use this approach, we ask questions that build a contextual understanding of fashion: when it comes to land, we can ask what fibers are indigenous to this region, rather than asking what's the most eco-friendly textile, which can lead to homogenization rather than regional biodiversity. When it comes to labor, we can home in on regional artisan practices and realize that fashion is art, and every garment worker is an artisan."

—Aditi Mayer, labor rights activist, photojournalist, and sustainable fashion blogger

The alternative to fast fashion is known as slow fashion, sustainable fashion, or ethical fashion. Slow fashion brands often better reflect the true cost of clothing and produce garments with the intention of minimizing harm to people and the planet during manufacturing. This can look different for every corporation but can include using recycled or regenerative fibers, having fair trade certification, enforcing garment worker safety standards and working only with ethical factories, upcycling fabrics, and having smaller collections or fewer changing seasons. Consumers seeking to reduce their environmental impact can opt for sustainably and ethically made fashion when buying new.

Since this is a book about intersectional environmentalism, we can't just stop at the suggestion to buy sustainable fashion without addressing the elephant in the room: there is a steep financial barrier to entry within the sustainable fashion industry. Accessibility concerns include:

* **COST:** You can easily find a shirt for under ten dollars at a fast fashion brand, while a similar shirt may cost double, triple, or even more than quadruple that amount at a sustainable apparel company. Not everyone can afford to buy pricier sustainable fashion items.
* **MANUFACTURING LIMITATIONS:** Because fast fashion has a higher demand than more costly sustainable alternatives, sustainable apparel brands have to pay higher premiums to obtain certifications and perform factory audits.
* **LACK OF INCLUSIVE SIZING:** Many sustainable fashion brands do not offer plus-size clothing, citing things like cost or lack of demand as a barrier. However, over 60 percent of American women wear a size 14 or above.[16]
* **THE GENTRIFICATION OF THRIFTING:** Shopping at thrift stores helps divert textiles away from landfills and

promotes reuse of clothing, and it's also been a way for lower-income families and individuals to have access to affordable clothing. With the rise of social media and the popularization of vintage items and thrifting, resellers have flocked to thrift stores to buy clothing at low prices to then mark up and resell online. This makes it harder for people who need to buy secondhand to do so.

GREEN ENERGY

RENEWABLE ENERGY, also known as clean or green energy, is derived from natural and renewable sources, like the sun and wind, as opposed to nonrenewable energy, which comes from finite sources, such as coal and oil. Some negative impacts of using nonrenewable energy sources are the destruction that occurs during extraction, the displacement of people who live in close proximity to the desired resource, pollution emitted during usage, and improper disposal into ecosystems. It is now well known that nonrenewable energy sources are a leading cause of environmental injustice, greenhouse gas emissions, and the climate crisis we are facing. What's less widely known is the painful and traumatic history involved with the implementation of green energy that continues to this day.

With innovation, green energy is becoming more affordable and accessible, and by 2025, renewable resources are forecasted to supply one-third of global energy needs.[17] Transitioning to green energy and infrastructure is one of the best solutions to reducing chemical emissions and environmental harm, and governments globally are aggressively pursuing this switch.

But while governments and corporations plan to transition to

119

renewable resources, Indigenous communities worldwide are being faced with the dark side of green energy: the lack of regard for their communities, their lack of inclusion within decision-making processes, and the constant threat of violence. If the global community does not act quickly to address these issues, marginalized people will be harmed by green energy transitions, because even renewable resources impact people and planet.

Indigenous communities are on the front lines of the fight for climate justice and renewable energy, but the expansion of green technology has introduced additional threats to their livelihoods. Jessie Cato, a program manager at the Business & Human Rights Resource Centre in Berlin, reported a "concerning rise" of human rights violations in the field of renewable energy, with over two hundred reports of displacement, threats, violence, and abuse spanning decades within Indigenous communities globally.[18]

BIOMASS ENERGY, BAN KHU, THAILAND

BIOMASS ENERGY is created from living or previously living things, such as trees, plant or animal material, sugarcane or corn crops, or even animal waste. With heat and combustion, biomass can generate electricity.[19]

A 2021 Reuters article detailed the shocking experience of Muhammad Lamoh, a resident of a small village in Ban Khu, Thailand. One day, local officials informed the residents of their plans to build a biomass plant in the community. The villagers did not consent to the development of the twenty-five-megawatt biomass plant because of concerns over its proximity to schools and its potential impacts on their health, and yet it started operating in 2020.

Shortly after the plant opened, community members noticed

strange smells, skin rashes, and a shortage of water from the canal that they used for their homes and for drinking, bathing, and agriculture.[20] They tried to alert the government but were left without support. Because adopting green energy is incentivized, these projects face less government and public scrutiny when implemented and are placed in communities regardless of their consent. Green energy projects must include the full consent of the surrounding communities that are being targeted for construction. Further, these projects should provide jobs, opportunities, and resources for members of the communities they're placed in.

✳

LITHIUM MINING, SOUTH AMERICA

LITHIUM IS an essential material for rechargeable batteries—from electric car batteries to those found in household electronics. With the push to create electric batteries that can power a new future of transportation and technology, the demand for lithium, a nonrenewable resource, has skyrocketed: in 2014 it cost $6,500 per metric ton, in 2016 it climbed to $9,000, and in 2020 it reached a whopping $17,000.[21] In a 2020 report, the World Bank forecasted that lithium production would need to increase by 500 percent by 2050 to meet the projected growing demand for green technology.[22]

Lithium is mined from the sand in a process that requires five hundred thousand gallons of water per ton of lithium extracted.[23] Miners drill deep holes in the sand and pump brine to the surface. After a year or more, the mineral can be collected after liquid evaporates. Around 70 percent of the world's lithium exists in South America, within Indigenous lands.[24] These lithium reserves are primarily concentrated in Argentina, Bolivia, and Chile, in an area referred to by the industry as the Lithium Triangle. Argentina has the

HOW DO LITHIUM-ION BATTERIES WORK?

A lithium-ion battery has three components: a positive electrode (+), a negative electrode (−), and a liquid (electrolyte) that exists between the + and the −. The positive electrode is often made from lithium iron phosphate (LiFePO4) or lithium cobalt oxide (LiCoO2); the negative electrode is made from carbon (graphite). When charged, ions move through the electrolytes, and electrons move in the opposite direction through the circuit. Lithium-ion batteries don't use heavy metals like mercury and can be recycled, and unlike simpler batteries, their charge and discharge can easily be regulated.

largest lithium reserves, followed by the Uyuni salt flats in Bolivia. Argentina has dozens of lithium projects in development, and as of 2018, Chile was the world's second-largest nation for lithium production.[25] Some refer to lithium as white gold because it's become one of the most sought-after minerals in the world.

The Atacama desert in northern Chile, home to the Indigenous Lickanantaí, or Atacama people, is the driest desert in the world and holds 40 percent of the world's lithium.[26] Two companies, SQM and Albemarle, control lithium production in Chile. Conflict between the Lickanantaí people and mining corporations dates back decades. Indigenous communities, fearful of decreasing water supply and quality, have advocated for better research and testing to ensure that quality meets health standards. In 2007, a coalition of Lickanantaí people and an official Indigenous governing body filed several lawsuits against SQM.[27] Many of their complaints centered around water scarcity and unauthorized water withdrawals by SQM and other lithium mining operations. SQM and Albemarle have led to less water replenishing the Atacama water table than what goes out; in fact, the water table loses 1,750 to 1,950 liters per second due to mining.[28]

In 2016, SQM damaged local ecosystems by going against established quotas and extracted more brine than the amount agreed upon. As a result, the Superintendence of the Environment started to issue sanctions.[29] SQM, looking to avoid losing its permit, put forth a $25 million plan to spearhead more environmental quality studies and improve their monitoring system; however, this plan was rejected by the Atacama Indigenous Council because it did not include provisions to repair the damage done. The Superintendence of the Environment ruled in favor of the Atacama Indigenous Council. In October 2019, protesters from Chile's Indigenous communities blocked off access to SQM's mining operations to show solidarity with the Chilean social justice protests and to take a stand against environmental degradation.[30]

In addition to the environmental concerns, corporations aren't investing enough funds and resources in the surrounding communities. In 2016, the *Washington Post* published an article that detailed how Minera Exar, a Canadian-Chilean lithium mining project expected to generate upward of $250 million per year in sales, paid the six surrounding Indigenous communities only $9,000 to $60,000 a year each, with some residents not even aware of that compensation.[31]

Lithium can also be mined in Australia and other parts of the world, with companies like Tesla testing out mining in the U.S. Some communities in the Lithium Triangle have been able to receive compensation and employment, but in order for these corporate interests to be truly just, Indigenous people in this area should receive even more employment opportunities, improved infrastructure, and compensation and be granted a seat at the table in decision-making processes. In addition to this, the social and environmental impacts of lithium extraction should be prioritized before companies scale up lithium production to achieve green tech goals.

WIND ENERGY, MEXICO

IN 2017, Mexico invested $6 billion in green energy (810 percent more than in 2016) and was among the top ten countries investing in renewable energy.[32]

One of those investments was the development of large wind farms in Oaxaca, Mexico, in the Isthmus of Tehuantepec. This region comprises the traditional lands of the Binnizá and Ikjoots Indigenous peoples (also known as Zapotecas and Huaves), who are dependent on the land for fishing and farming and who hold it sacred—all of which can be threatened by the wind farm infrastructure. In 2015, there were more than fifteen private wind power projects in this region, with a total megawatt capacity of around 2,007 (of the total 33,200-megawatt potential of the area).[33] Some of this electricity is used for companies in the area and some of it is sold for usage in urban areas.

Opposition to wind projects in Oaxaca dates to 1994 and has increased through the decades. In 2006, a 369-megawatt solar project by Mareña Renovables (now known as Eólica del Sur) was proposed to provide electricity to large beverage compa-

HOW DOES WIND ENERGY WORK?

If a regular oscillating household fan uses electricity to make wind, wind turbines do the opposite: they use the wind to generate electricity. Naturally occurring wind moves the blades of the giant "fan" of a wind turbine around a rotor, similar to a propeller, and energy is created as the generator spins. Wind turbines harness this energy and turn it into electricity.

nies. In 2009, Environmental Impact Assessments indicated a real threat of biodiversity loss due to the project, as well as the potential instigation of social conflict within the surrounding Indigenous communities. However, the Mexican government was in favor of the project as it fit within its push for a green economy.[34] In 2012, the project was successfully stopped due to protests and organizing by the surrounding San Dionisio community, which was fearful of the project's impact on fishing and farming and concerned that it required construction in a lagoon considered sacred to the local Indigenous community.

This successful effort led to more support of Indigenous communities and the formation of the People's Assembly of Álvaro Obregón and a separate community-led police force to defend the land.[35] This resistance, although successful at blocking some projects, was met with both scrutiny and violence from the government and corporations in support of expanding green tech. In July 2018, after leaving a community policing shift, activist Rolando Crispin López, who fought for the protection of Indigenous communities for years and against the wind projects, was murdered by a municipal police officer in a drive-by motorcycle shooting.[36]

This violence has only escalated since, as tension grows between the government, corporations, and activists. In 2020, activists who opposed the wind power project were ambushed by a group with alleged links to a local crime boss at a coronavirus checkpoint, where fifteen people were violently murdered at gunpoint and even more were injured. Two of the victims were women protesting the abuses of members of the government, including one of the suspected attackers.[37]

The global transition to green energy should not come at the expense of the safety of Indigenous peoples. We urgently need to phase out our reliance on nonrenewable resources, and green tech should be highly prioritized as a solution. However, within an intersectional approach to environmentalism, we must acknowledge the dark side of green energy and the harm that these initiatives have caused to marginalized communities. We must also ensure that future projects take the protection of all people into consideration. We don't have to choose between justice for people and the planet. Social justice and a green economy can and should coexist.

Q: What can be done to correct the green tech industry's impact on Indigenous people and the planet?

"Wildfires that create sterile soils are one example of the consequence of excluding Indigenous peoples; Indigenous guardianship, the application of Traditional Ecological Knowledge (TEK), and land back are all essential in the effort to reverse the impacts of climate change. When Indigenous communities tell you to take action, listen and be an active ally, understanding that another community's fight is also your own. Engage and develop a personal responsibility to conserve earth for the next seven generations. Listen to the diverse perspectives of Indigenous peoples and learn about their cultures, traditions, and battles for people + planet."

—Andrea Perez, Indigenous environmental justice advocate and geospatial analyst

VEGANISM/PLANT-BASED LIVING

WHAT WE eat impacts not only our health but the environment and how we contribute to global emissions. A study from Oxford University found that an individual's food-based carbon footprint can be reduced by up to 73 percent if they remove meat and dairy from their diet.[38] Even participating in Meatless Mondays (no meat for one day a week) can reduce an individual's carbon footprint by 7.5 pounds of CO_2.[39] This study found that if everyone globally stopped eating meat and dairy products, global farmland use could be reduced by 75 percent, an area the size of China, Australia, the U.S., and the EU combined![40] A 2019 report by the Intergovernmental Panel on Climate Change found that both agriculture and forestry have contributed almost a quarter of global greenhouse gas emissions.[41] Livestock, or animal agriculture, contributes a whopping 14.5 percent of the planet's greenhouse gas emissions.[42]

From 2014 to 2017, there was a 600 percent increase in the U.S. of people identifying as vegans (from 1 percent to 6 percent); in the UK over the past decade, a 350 percent increase; and in Portugal, a 400 percent increase in the last decade.[43] Global Google Trends search data also shows an increase in veganism searches worldwide, with top locations being Israel, Australia, Canada, Austria, and New Zealand. Research predicts that China's vegan market will grow more than 17 percent from 2015 to 2050, and in 2016, the Chinese health ministry guidelines encouraged the nation of over one billion people to reduce its meat consumption by 50 percent by 2030.[44]

People gravitate toward plant-based, vegetarian, and vegan diets and lifestyles for a variety of reasons. I'll focus mainly on the environment in this chapter, but spirituality, religion, ethics, health, animal rights, income, environment, and preference are just a few of the reasons people choose not to consume meat. Regardless of individual motivations, plant-based eating is on the rise globally, and there's no doubt that this trend has positive implications for the environment.

REASONS FOR EATING MEAT LESS, RARELY, OR NEVER

(Asked of those who are eating less meat or who rarely or never eat meat)
Would you say each of the following is a **Major Reason**, a **Minor Reason**, or **Not a Reason** why you have been eating less meat / rarely eat meat / do not eat meat?

Major Reason	Minor Reason	Not a Reason	
70%		20%	10%	Concern about your health
49%	21%	30%	Concern about the environment
43%	22%	34%	Concern about food safety
41%	24%	35%	Concern about animal welfare
15%	19%	64%	You see a lot of other people doing it
12%	17%	72%	Religious reasons
16%	24%	59%	Convenience because other family members are eating less meat / rarely eat meat / do not eat meat

A 2019 Gallup Poll on the reasons people reduced meat consumption in the U.S.[45]

LACK OF REPRESENTATION

NOW THAT plant-based eating is becoming more mainstream, it's important to consider what voices are being heard and elevated in this space. When you google "vegan" or turn to social media to learn more about veganism, representation of people of color is scarce. This trend carries over into documentary and film projects, social media influencers selected for partnerships, and how veganism is represented in education, environmental movements, and media. The lack of representation is concerning and doesn't reflect reality;

communities of color have practiced plant-based lifestyles for centuries, and in the modern day have actually adopted plant-based lifestyles at higher than average rates. A Pew Research Center study found that 8 percent of Black Americans identify as strict vegans or vegetarians, as opposed to 3 percent of the general population.[46] A 2020 Gallup poll found that people of color in the U.S. reported reducing their meat consumption at a much higher rate than white Americans (31 percent versus 19 percent).[47]

When we look globally, the countries with the largest increase of vegetarian populations between 2016 and '17 are (ranked from highest growth to lowest) Nigeria, Pakistan, Indonesia, the Philippines, Germany, Brazil, Turkey, Kenya, Thailand, and Italy. Many of these countries are in the Global South, although mainstream representation of plant-based diets is largely centered around perspectives from the Global North.[48]

These countries have the most vegetarians overall per capita: India (31 to 42 percent), Mexico (19 percent), Brazil (14 percent), Taiwan (14 percent), Switzerland (13 percent), Israel (10.3 percent), New Zealand (10 percent), Sweden (10 percent), Canada (9.4 percent), U.S. (5 to 8 percent), and Russia (3 to 4 percent).[49] Three out of the top five countries are concentrated in the Global South, and while the U.S.'s vegan population is growing, it has a significantly smaller vegan population per capita than the top countries. This isn't a competition, but it's important to take the facts into account when considering which narratives around plant-based lifestyles, reduction of meat consumption, and veganism and vegetarianism are amplified and given a platform.

When I searched "vegan documentaries" on Google, I found that the top thirty results featured either a white narrator or a primarily white cast, and that most of the documentaries had been made in the U.S. or UK. Some of the stories also felt historically incomplete, with narratives focused on the "newness" of veganism or plant-based living, even though the earliest records of vegetarianism date back to ancient India. The problem with centering primarily white, wealthy vegan perspectives from the Global North is that this approach fails to acknowledge the pioneers of this practice and their reasons for their choice, and it doesn't credit these populations with reducing their environmental footprint (for decades and sometimes centuries!). Even if the vegetarianism that dates back to ancient India predates the climate crisis, India's more than 30 percent vegetarian population is contributing positively to the health of the environment with this choice. Instead of rebranding solutions from a Western perspective, environmentalists should seek to amplify the cultural practices of BIPOC communities globally and also give them credit for inspiring the ideas for what modern veganism and vegetarianism look like in the first place.

The term "veganism" was coined by British woodworker Donald Watson in 1944 to make a distinction between vegetarians who consumed animal products (like dairy) and those who did not.[50] He later went on to found the Vegan Society to further promote vegan lifestyles, which gained mainstream traction in the 2000s. While Watson did coin the term "veganism" and helped popularize it, vegan ideologies could be found in Eastern religions like Jainism, Buddhism, and Hinduism for centuries prior to 1944. The concept of cruelty-free eating can also be found in the Ital diet of Rastafarians, which encourages consuming plant-based and unprocessed foods.[51]

The lack of representation of BIPOC within the mainstream vegan movement follows the same pattern that other non-intersectional environmentalists have perpetuated: the lack of prioritization and consideration of Black, Latinx, Indigenous, Asian, and people of color's perspectives and cultural values and the lack of advocacy of their civil rights within the context of environmentalism. "Anti-Blackness is wholly embedded in the system of white, 'mainstream veganism,'" reported LoriKim Alexander, an organizer of the Brooklyn-based Black VegFest, in a 2020 interview with Civil Eats.[52]

The anti-Blackness that Alexander referenced has fueled conflict within the vegan movement for decades and stems from the lack of intersectional perspectives. Many BIPOC vegans and vegetarians view veganism not as a single issue driven by animal suffering but as a confluence of several points of identity. While concerns about animal welfare can motivate veganism, as shown in the earlier chart, there can be other drivers that overlap with identity, which for many can cause a disconnect. For example, if people are driven to practice plant-based eating because of cultural values and religion, their veganism might be closely tied to their cultural identity—especially if they come from a marginalized and historically excluded group. If people are drawn to veganism for ethical reasons or health concerns that are unrelated to cultural identity, they might not consider other pathways to veganism and their value

For example, a driver of veganism can also be the protection of human lives because people are also animals. Thus, advocacy for social justice and the liberation of marginalized people is also related to the protection of animals and the environment. BIPOC perspectives matter, and these nuances should be explored to advocate for inclusion and equity within the plant-based conversation.

"Vegans can become intersectional in their work by recognizing the history of extractive systems stemming from environmental colonialism. To attempt to dismantle extractive systems like factory farms is to be anti-capitalistic, as industrial factory farms are focused on GDP maximum growth. Recognizing that the abuse of both humans and nonhuman animals is not rooted in the idea of human supremacy, but rather white supremacy as it has created hierarchical oppressive roles in the way we treat living beings. Non-intersectional veganism is dangerous as it further reinforces colonial mindsets of blaming individuals vs. the system that allowed oppressive systems to flourish. We must be specific in how we characterize movements and understand that fighting for total liberation includes both humans and nonhuman animals."

—ISAIAS HERNANDEZ, creator of Queer Brown Vegan

THE IE PLEDGE BREAKOUT AND CONCLUSION:

I will amplify the messages of Black, Indigenous, and POC activists and environmental leaders. I will not remain silent during pivotal political and cultural moments that impact Black, Indigenous, and POC communities and all marginalized identities.

This tenet of the pledge is one of the most important. It's twofold: it encourages you to 1) amplify the messages of diverse climate leaders and activists *and* 2) not remain silent. Silence is what allows the status quo to continue. Together all of our voices are so powerful—much more powerful than we might think. Take it from me: I truly didn't think one post on social media—one small moment of resistance— would catapult intersectional environmentalism into existence and allow me to dedicate my life to environmental education.

Amplification is important because it leads to a ripple effect of awareness that can shift into action and change the world. Sometimes people downplay the importance of raising awareness, but amplification is one of the easiest and most powerful ways to draw attention to narratives and causes that need visibility. Every leader is just a person, just like you. Leaders were individuals who were listened to, one person at a time, until a community and the momentum of grassroots activism allowed their voices to be elevated.

My unique experiences in activism and digital media have made me realize just how powerful our individual actions are, and how they can lead to systemic change. Each of us is a participant in a global ecosystem, and we have the potential to make a greener, safer, and more equitable future for everyone through what we choose to amplify and put action behind. Activism is for everyone. Don't let anyone make you doubt yourself. We can all play a role—no matter how big or small.

So think about your special skills and apply them to the movements you care about. Even though I'm anxious and don't always feel comfortable holding a megaphone, I have found that writing and digital media are ways for me to contribute my unique skills to environmentalism. Your activism may not look like mine, or like the next person's, but all of our strengths are pieces of the puzzle. A mentor of mine once said, "Even the revolution needs accountants." This made me laugh, but it's true! We can each contribute our skills in some way.

So I'll leave you with this: I hope you understand how powerful you are. Please do share and amplify the messages you believe the world needs to hear. Take a leap of faith and attend a local protest if you can. Raise your hand to introduce an intersectional perspective where it needs to be heard. Stand up for what's right and don't back down, even when it's difficult, even when you might feel alone, because trust me: we're out there. There are generations of intersectional environmentalists in the field and a community that's ready to embrace you with support. Together, we can transform the future of environmentalism and, with collective action, spread our message across the globe and change enough hearts and minds to positively alter the future.

The future is intersectional.

TOOL KIT

HERE ARE some further resources from activists around the world to help you take action, deepen your understanding of intersectional environmentalism, and continue on your environmental journey. The below excerpts are collected from one-on-one interviews and questionnaires conducted with each participant for inclusion in this book.

THE INTERSECTIONAL ENVIRONMENTALIST CHEAT SHEET Q&A WITH GLOBAL ENVIRONMENTALISTS

ON THE NEED FOR DIVERSITY, EQUITY, AND INCLUSION IN THE ENVIRONMENTAL MOVEMENT:

✳ **MIKAELA LOACH,** climate justice activist and cohost of

the *Yikes* podcast: The nature of the organizing I've been involved with has to do with challenging powerful systems. In challenging these systems, I've also been challenged myself. I've been challenged on my understanding of "diversity and inclusion." I now recognize that inclusion in a harmful system should never be the goal. In many ways, representation politics can embolden harmful institutions by allowing them to continue to exist. Instead, I want my organizing work to demolish old systems and build new ones. I want collective liberation, not simply diversity in who gets to be the oppressor.

✳ **VANESSA NAKATE, climate justice activist and founder of the Rise Up movement, Uganda:** Climate justice is only justice if it includes all of us. Erasing the voices of African and Black activists means erasing our stories, erasing our experiences, erasing the challenges that we are going through. We are the least responsible for the climate crisis but we are definitely among the most affected by climate change. Climate justice is racial justice. Environmental justice starts with listening to the most affected people and communities.

✳ **KRISTY DRUTMAN, digital strategist and host of *Brown Girl Green*:** I work to create conversations rooted in culture, heritage, and struggle—to provide healing, community, and empowerment for BIPOC who have not been recognized or acknowledged in this space for their contributions for far too long. Diversity in this space is not just nice to have; it can be the difference between life and death for many communities around the world today.

ON HONORING ELDER ENVIRONMENTAL JUSTICE ACTIVISTS IN OUR WORK:

✳ **WANJIKU (WAWA) GATHERU, environmental justice advocate and founder of Black Girl Environmentalist:** Learn the expansive history of the environmental justice movement and the untold stories of our elders, and always provide active gratitude to the elders that have given us the language of progress that we rely on in imagining a just climate future. We are because of them.

✳ **AYANA ALBERTINI-FLEURANT, co-executive director and director of policy and programming at Generation Green:** Intergenerational organizing and activism are crucial to a successful movement in the Black environmental space. The pioneers and elders of the EJ movement were revolutionaries, longtime activists, and scholars who started a movement that for the first time called for acknowledgment, assessment, and accountability for environmental problems in our communities. EJ elders also constructed a holistic definition of "environment" that is relevant to the Black environmental experience. We will always uplift and learn from and attribute the foundation of Black environmentalism to the incredible leaders who have dedicated their lives to spearheading this fight for generations to come.

ON HONORING INDIGENOUS CULTURE AND TRADITIONS IN THE ENVIRONMENTAL MOVEMENT:

✳ **ANDREA PEREZ, Indigenous environmental justice advocate and geospatial analyst:** Center Indigenous autonomy: it precedes exploitation by extraction and desecration of the land's natural resources. Clean energy units have historically been placed near marginalized communities and disrupt sensitive ecosystems. Communities need to be included in the decision to install clean energy instead of placing clean energy systems in the "path of least resistance," much like the oil and gas industry. Lower societal consumption of energy + resources to benefit people + planet.

✳ **JORDAN MARIE DANIEL, founder of Rising Hearts:** The current environmental movement can honor Indigenous culture and traditions by creating space to incorporate their voices, traditional knowledge, caretaking of the lands, and practices in all discussions and organizing, and across platforms. Indigenous people have been caretakers of the lands for generations and we protect up to 86 percent of the world's global biodiversity while we make up only 5 percent of the world's population. Indigenous voices must be part of the processes and pathways of what justice, accountability, restoration, and healing look like as we move toward collaborative and intersectional approaches for a just transition for all people and the planet.

ON BEING INCLUSIVE OF DISABILITY REPRESENTATION:

✳ **AMBIKA RAJYAGOR, intersectional feminist and disabled rights advocate, cofounder of Disabled & Outdoors:** Eco-ableism creates a divide that "others" disabled environmentalists—and considering the fact that at least 15 percent of the world's population lives with a disability, this is counterproductive to the idea of being an inclusive movement. Allies to the disabled environmentalist community should help advocate for accessible sustainable practices and materials that are considerate of disabled needs. When holding panels, writing legislation, building sustainable programs, and creating materials that are helpful to the environment, it is very important that the disabled community is not only advocated for but also represented.

✳ **LARISSA CRAWFORD, founder of Future Ancestors Services:** Environmentalism that fails to account for the ways that climate change amplifies barriers faced by people with disabilities does not and cannot lead to climate justice. Environmentalism that produces "solutions" and spaces that actively cause further harm to people with disabilities does not and cannot lead to climate justice.

ON HOW STUDENTS CAN GET INVOLVED IN CLIMATE WORK:

✳ **ANUSHKA BHASKAR, founder of Avritah and the HEAL Program:** Know that there is always a place for you in this movement because this movement is for you. To help you find your place in the movement, start with what you love. This means that you first must take the time to discover what it is that you love (in my opinion, a truly revolutionary act). Joining the climate movement has been, for me, an act of self-discovery.

✳ **KIANA KAZEMI, environmental justice activist and cofounder of Circularity:** As youth activists, the future we fight for is for everyone, one in which we are free of today's binaries and oppressive systems, one in which youth no longer have to fight for their future. This is why our fight must include the voices of every community and every perspective. We need artists, educators, engineers, scientists, writers, mechanics…We need everyone to center environmental justice in their work, so that we can collectively create this future.

ON USING PRIVILEGE TO ADVOCATE FOR PEOPLE AND THE PLANET:

✳ **PHIL AIKEN, cofounder of Intersectional Environmentalist and host of *just to save the world*:** Stand up to those in power when it is necessary, shut up when it's time to listen to those most affected by systems of oppression, and speak up when your white peers are harming others with their ignorance. Without dismantling white supremacy and achieving environmental justice for all people, we cannot reverse climate change and build a regenerative future.

✳ **SABS KATZ, cofounder of Intersectional Environmentalist and social activist:** First is just taking time to really, genuinely listen. Not to argue, not to debate people's lived experiences, not to share fragility or try to defend yourself for the privileges you hold. White supremacy is like a poison—you have to purge it before you can get towards a place of healing. That purging is never comfortable but it must be done to move forward and understand the many injustices BIPOC face.

ON SUPPORTING A MORE INCLUSIVE OUTDOORS INDUSTRY AND EQUITY IN NATURE:

✳ **TERESA BAKER, founder of the Outdoor CEO Diversity Pledge and founder of the In Solidarity Project:** We can no longer accept doing things the old ways, as the only way (polite and with permission). We must be open to listening and applying strategies that are brought to us by community leaders. That is where change happens: in communities with thought leaders and "solutionaries" leading the way.

✳ **EVELYNN ESCOBAR, founder and executive director of Hike Clerb:** Part of our struggle as people of color is that we live in a world full of systems that try to suppress who we actually are. When we look inward and have that time to reflect, we are able to tap into the raw personal power each and every one of us holds. That power is something nature can help us to see. We have an inherent tie to the land that extends back to our ancestors and to us today, as a living, breathing part of nature. Equity in this space is absolutely crucial because it allows us to envision a world for ourselves beyond what we are conditioned to believe. It allows us to connect to a source, to heal generational trauma, to release, to play, to experience joy, and most importantly to get in touch with our essence.

ON KEEPING THE FOCUS ON CLIMATE OPTIMISM AND SOLUTIONS:

✳ **SOPHIA LI, multimedia journalist and cohost of *All of the Above*:** Climate optimism plays a role in our fight for an equitable future because the movement must start internally: if we have a fearful relationship with Mother Nature, we quickly burn out—fear isn't sustainable long term for a true global liberation to a greener future. A symbiotic relationship with Mother Nature rooted in love and abundance (as Indigenous communities have always practiced), however, is the sustainable answer.

✳ **PHIL AIKEN, cofounder of Intersectional Environmentalist and host of *just to save the world*:** My best piece of advice for anyone that wants to use their unique passions and skills to add to the movement is to root their actions in love, not fear, and focus their energy on the solutions, not the problems. A solution-based mindset helps me sustain my own passion for the work and momentum toward positive change.

✳ **TERESA BAKER, founder of the Outdoor CEO Diversity Pledge and founder of the In Solidarity Project:** Raise your voices and keep raising them until power structures begin to listen and adhere to your messages. Silent demands can never be heard; demand out loud. If you have a message and that message is fair, be a nuisance: do not accept NO as the final answer. I want future generations to be able to look back at those of us who are currently paving the way and think to themselves, "Because of them, I too can make a difference."

ON EFFECTIVELY SHARING INFORMATION WITH MY COMMUNITY THROUGH EDUCATION:

✳ **JOSÉ GONZÁLEZ, founder and director emeritus of Latino Outdoors:** Education is not merely information sharing, so as a teacher one must consider a fuller range of how people learn and how that can be impacted. Ultimately, it is about how we engage with people's mental models, their cognitive maps, which can contain erroneous information, but if we approach it purely from a punitive approach, it does not open up the space for interest, engagement, and ultimately the inclusion of new information.

✳ **ISAIAS HERNANDEZ, creator of Queer Brown Vegan:** Education is one of the first steps to becoming aware or learning more about social, racial, or environmental injustices. It's also a powerful tool to allow us to examine how policies and practices have harmed Black, Indigenous, and people of color. Environmental education is a human right and it should not be an uncomfortable topic for educators to teach how race, class, and gender intersect with our environment.

✳ **PINAR SINOPOULOS-LLOYD AND SO SINOPOULOS-LLOYD, cofounders of Queer Nature:** Environmental curriculums must foreground Indigenous histories across the Americas in addition to centering and amplifying current water/land protector movements of ongoing Indigenous resistance. It's important that these are told from Native perspectives, especially from Indigenous women, Indigequeers, and two-spirit kin who are at the forefront of these movements.

ON HOW BIPOC AND MARGINALIZED COMMUNITIES ARE TIED TO ENVIRONMENTALISM:

✳ **SOPHIA LI, multimedia journalist and cohost of *All of the Above*:** The #StopAsianHate movement is directly tied to our fight against the systems of oppression that hurt the environment because they are the *same* systems: vulnerable communities are all oppressed by the institutions of white supremacy, white nationalism, and capitalism.

✳ **SABS KATZ, cofounder of Intersectional Environmentalist and social activist:** *Tikkun olam* is a Hebrew phrase which means "repair the world." It means we are responsible for making the world a better place than when we got here. We are encouraged to fight against injustice because we too have been victims. Whether that means treating Mama Earth with respect or fighting for equal rights, Judaism teaches us not to sit idly by when we are faced with oppressive systems.

ON HOW EVERYDAY INDUSTRIES, SUCH AS FASHION AND HEALTH, ARE TIED TO ENVIRONMENTALISM AND HUMAN RIGHTS:

✳ **ADITI MAYER, labor rights activist, photojournalist, and sustainable fashion blogger:** In order to build an intersectional future for ethical fashion—one that doesn't exploit garment workers and the environment—I think it's helpful to begin by thinking of fashion as a product of land and labor, and reorienting our relationship to both of those things. When we use this approach, we ask questions that build a contextual understanding of fashion: when it comes to land, we can ask what fibers are indigenous to this region, rather than asking what's the most eco-friendly textile, which can lead to homogenization rather than regional biodiversity. When it comes to labor, we can home in on regional artisan practices and realize that fashion is art, and every garment worker is an artisan.

✳ **ANUSHKA BHASKAR, founder of Avritah and the HEAL Program:** One main intersection between health and environmental justice is that when systemic problems result in environmental injustices, they don't just result in an imbalanced and sick environment; they also cause negative health outcomes, which usually manifest *first* within the most underserved communities, eventually affecting people of all demographics. Health inequities emerge when vulnerable communities are exposed to poor environmental quality and as a result experience more sickness and disease than wealthier, less polluted communities. Compounded by the cracks in global and domestic health care systems, these issues are devastating the health of generations of people.

Many underrepresented groups such as BIPOC, LGBTQIA+, and low-income communities already are disproportionately impacted by the climate crisis and other environmental problems, but also struggle with inadequate access to and poor-quality health care.

ON TAKING DIGITAL ACTIVISM TO REAL LIFE AND GETTING INVOLVED IN POLICY:

✳ **MIKAELA LOACH, climate justice activist and cohost of the *Yikes* podcast:** We can't let social media distract us with numbers and likes, leading us to build movements which are mile-wide but only inch-deep (refer to Adrienne Maree Brown's work for more on this). We need to use social media as a launchpad to get folks into deep learning—beyond infographics—which will cause deep, meaningful, actionable change.

✳ **JORDAN CHATMAN, brand strategist and multimedia environmentalist:** Create spaces that bring like-minded individuals together (even if it's just you and your friends/ family), collect and share empirical data, participate in local meetings, and hold your city officials accountable.

ON BIPOC RECLAIMING NATURE FOR THEMSELVES:

✳ **RON GRISWELL, founder and executive director of HBCUs Outside:** My advice to a young Black environmentalist looking to take their first adventure and reclaim nature for themselves is to first recognize that we belong in these spaces just as much as anyone. Second, no matter the fear, anxiety, or discomfort, having the ability to operate outside of our comfort zone is one of the most important aspects for beginning any new adventure, along with allowing our curiosity to lead and entering into nature with a heart full of respect for the land. And in reclaiming nature for ourselves, it's important that we expand and redefine the outdoors.

✳ **JOSÉ GONZÁLEZ, founder and director emeritus of Latino Outdoors:** There are many unnamed elders and heroes in this work, along with contemporary peers. To do them justice would be to have a LONG and ongoing list. Still, some names to start include Ynés Enriquetta Julietta Mexía, Ralph Abascal, Dolores Huerta, Emma Tenayuca, Arturo Sandoval, Juan Martinez, Omar Gallardo, Marce Gutiérrez-Graudiņš, and all of the Latino Outdoors leaders, past and present.

ON MAKING SURE OUR ACTIVISM DOESN'T FOCUS ON JUST THE GLOBAL NORTH BUT ON OTHER COUNTRIES THAT ARE MORE IMPACTED BY THE CLIMATE CRISIS:

✳ **VANESSA NAKATE, climate justice activist and founder of the Rise Up movement, Uganda:** If the media and the climate community do not tell our stories, then we will not be able to get the justice that we deserve. Every activist has a story to tell, every story has a solution to give, and every solution has a life to change.

✳ **ABIGAIL ADEKUNBI THOMAS, environmentalist, Environmental Employee Engagement at Patagonia:** Western countries, and various global corporations, continue to exploit many African countries by transferring waste, pollution, and environmental degradation to the continent. Every African country is different, with their own unique climate challenges, but ultimately, these environmental impacts will have and already have disproportionate health, economic, and environmental impacts throughout the continent, especially for low-income and rural communities.

✳ **HILDA F. NAKABUYE, activist and founder of Uganda's Fridays for Future movement:** We have lost most of it to leaders' selfish gains, industrialization, and timber business. Also, pollution. In my country, Uganda, we are blessed with over five lakes and multiple rivers, but many people can't access water. One [lake] of which being Lake Victoria, which is the biggest freshwater body in Africa and the second in the world, but its levels are reducing at a high rate; among other effects are pollution. Research shows it will be dried up one hundred years from now. Its waters are becoming greener and thicker, often making it unsafe for domestic use and existence of aquatic life. This is why I think Black activists' perspectives need to be included and recognized. Black activists are often ignored in the climate change debate, yet they are on the front lines and experiencing climate change effects firsthand. Currently, my country, Uganda, is left with only 8 percent forest cover. This puts them in a position where they can draw on their experiences [and] share their stories to create solutions to combat the climate crisis.

✳ **BEATRICE TULAGAN, climate organizer, the Philippines:** Climate impacts in the Philippines are not just headlines about the last drought or the last typhoon. The climate story here is not just about disasters. We have environmentalists going up against fossil fuel companies who are silenced, threatened, and murdered; women and LGBTQ+ people attacked and violated in the aftermath of disasters in evacuation centers; communities complaining of health problems due to coal projects; climate justice activists being red-tagged by a government that doesn't bat an eyelash at human rights violations; and Indigenous groups robbed of land by corporations. We're facing injustices here day in and day out, wrought and exacerbated by climate change and its impacts in every imaginable way, from economics to human rights. But we also hold solutions and a great narrative of resistance.

ON WHAT IT MEANS TO TRULY ACHIEVE CLIMATE JUSTICE:

✳ **LARISSA CRAWFORD, founder of Future Ancestors Services:** Environmentalism cannot be equitable or sustainable without climate justice; the physical consequences of environmental and climate change cannot be removed from the social and political implications and causes. I have been taught that climate justice means that climate action done on any of the globe's Indigenous lands must center Indigenous peoples, knowledge systems, and sovereignty, and the lived experiences of and barriers to equity-seeking groups. Climate justice is also intrinsically tied to the decolonization of Indigenous identities and the recognition of African indigeneity. The strength of our ability to connect with ancestors, land, and our inherent Indigenous rights is a determinant of environmental sustainability.

✳ **PINAR SINOPOULOS-LLOYD AND SO SINOPOULOS-LLOYD, cofounders of Queer Nature:** Teaching multispecies kinship practices such as naturalist interpretation, wildlife tracking, nature-inspired art, and other place-based skills are forms of building intimacy and accountability with place and with other species, as well as healing the understated problem of species isolation. We feel it is critical to engage these various forms of emergent and embodied learning and not solely generate our land ethic through interaction with data and pre-given narratives about environmentalism. Interrupting human supremacy looks like building relationships with other than human species through reciprocal kinship—what we refer to as Ayni in Quechua. Many Indigenous cosmologies emphasize kincentric (relationship-centered) ecological ethics (see work by Indigenous ecologists Enrique Salmón, Dennis Martinez, Robin Wall Kimmerer), and it is something we should work to center more in environmental justice.

✳ **AYANA ALBERTINI-FLEURANT, co–executive director and director of policy and programming at Generation Green:** Environmental liberation has an Afrocentric lens and sees Blackness through the lens of decolonial border thinking. It centers both Afro-Indigeneity and ancestral ways of knowing alongside Afro-futuristic visions of Black people thriving all throughout the Black diaspora. Environmental liberation transcends the confines of the bureaucratic neoliberal state "justice" by identifying the North Star of the EL movement: making sure that Black people can be liberated and thrive in their environments.

✳ **KEVIN J. PATEL, youth climate activist and founder and executive director of OneUpAction:** The environmental movement as a whole must adopt strategies that explicitly seek to protect the interests of darker-skin-tone people of color and in general people of color (BIPOC). Let's make not only overt racism socially unacceptable, but covert racism [should] also be made socially unacceptable, because this is what has led the environmental movement to be white-centered. Education and acknowledgment of colorism can be strong forces for dismantling skin-tone bias—and

151

help promote healing for those within the environmental movement experiencing it.

ON HOW CREATIVES, ARTISTS, AND STORYTELLERS PLAY AN ACTIVE ROLE:

* **WYN WILEY / PATTIE GONIA, queer environmentalist:**
Creatives play a vital role in the climate movement. They are often the people communicating key research, data, and action points through their art forms of photography, videography, writing, design, social media, and more. It's often the role of creatives to access and synthesize that information and share it in formats that are equally accessible for all. So I believe that the climate movement story must be told, TikTok'd, Instagrammed, memed, and most of all *shared* with our diverse communities through storytelling that meets our communities where they are at and helps us all understand complex climate issues through creative communication solutions.

* **MING D. LIU, climate communicator and head of PR at Intersectional Environmentalist:** The environmental movement needs everyone. Public relations and communications play a leading role in the movement: it influences how people see the climate crisis and what they understand of it. In order to build a more intersectional environmental movement, we need to ensure that climate communications focus on shifting the narrative to tell the stories that aren't amplified or highlighted and explore deeper than just the surface level, since climate issues are so intrinsically connected to social and racial justice.

ON HOW BIPOC FOLX CAN NAVIGATE AND ADVOCATE FOR THEMSELVES IN THE ENVIRONMENTAL MOVEMENT:

✳ **KAMIJAH JOURNET, marketing strategist and board director at Runners for Public Lands:** I often wish there was a road map for how to show up in spaces where the faces don't look like ours, but I would be remiss if I said that I had it figured out. I've been one of few Black faces in the outdoors and environmental movement my entire life, but I often remind myself that I'm not alone. If you care about the planet and advocate for its protection, you are an environmentalist. You deserve space to speak, to share, and to be a part of this movement as much as anyone else. So I advise young Black environmentalists to remind themselves of that fact, and to share that sentiment with those who need a reminder too.

✳ **WANJIKU (WAWA) GATHERU, environmental justice advocate and founder of Black Girl Environmentalist:** Black girls and women are constantly propped up as martyrs of superhuman strength, with the will and power to hold the weight of the world upon our shoulders. Yes, we are magic, but we also are human. Lean into your morality and prioritize spaces in this movement that validate not only your existence but your future. While we should never feel shamed for our capacity to love without return, we shouldn't have to give up our livelihoods in the process. There are so many people in this movement that are willing and excited to build a movement made in the image of all of us. Seek them out and grow in community with them.

✳ **TERESA BAKER, founder of the Outdoor CEO Diversity Pledge and founder of the In Solidarity Project:** We must not be afraid to speak up. The power structures in place applaud our silence. We must act with intent and not shy away when we are faced with opposition. If your voice shakes, raise it anyway. If your body shivers, be firm in your posture. No matter how scared we become, we must be vigilant in our efforts around environmental protection. We can no longer afford to wait for other saviors. We are more than capable of standing in support of one another and forging ahead in our commitment to the planet and one another. If not us, why? We can no longer ask the question of who.

Q&A FROM THE IE COMMUNITY

THE INTERSECTIONAL Environmentalist platform began as an online community on social media during the summer of 2020 (@intersectionalenvironmentalist). I asked three questions:

WHAT IS AN INTERSECTIONAL ENVIRONMENTALIST ISSUE THAT ISN'T TALKED ABOUT ENOUGH?

* **THE IMPACT** of health on low income communities. —Devanshi, San Francisco, CA
* **THE IMPACT** of bottle bills and plastic bag bans on people experiencing homelessness. —Jenna, Willimantic, CT
* **FOOD SECURITY** and how it intersects with environmental choices. —Shelby, Minneapolis, MN
* **NATURAL DISASTER** impacts on poverty, affordability of sustainable products. —Dani, USA
* **CENTERING INDIGENOUS** people, every conversation should mention them. —Jitterbug Art, USA

✴ **PROTECTIONS REVERSED** for the Tongass; threatens Indigenous subsistence. Tongass is also vital for carbon sequestration and holds 44 percent of CO_2 across national forests, and Alaska is warming at 2–3 times the rate of the lower forty-eight. This impacts Indigenous resources. —Jess, AK and TX

✴ **SUSTAINABLE, EQUITABLE** urban planning. —Grace, Chicago, IL

✴ **THE URBAN** heat island effect's impact on underserved communities. —Tanner, Brantley, VA

✴ **THE UNEQUAL** access to water resources. —Maddie, Tingle, NJ

✴ **THE BIAS** of international fisheries law and how it disregards/fails global south countries and communities. —Leanne, UK

✴ **BIODIVERSITY LOSS;** people still don't realize how much of an impact loss of flora and fauna can create. —Gunjhan, Dehradun, India

✴ **GOING BEYOND** U.S.-based examples and centering U.S.-based narratives. —Leena, London, UK

✴ **INTERSECTIONALITY OF** the climate crisis and the outdoor industry. —Marie, Bellingham, WA

✴ **ACCESSIBLE, STYLISH,** and affordable fashion for disabled people. —Rebecca, New York, NY

✴ **THE EFFECT** of the climate crisis on people with disabilities. —Sarah, Hill, CT

✴ **HOW TO** remedy the potential loss of jobs from transitioning to a green economy. —Eric Johnson, St. Louis, MO

✴ **AN ENVIRONMENTAL** justice issue that is not talked about enough or rather just talked about very performatively is the systemic issue of colorism. Too often the conversations that occur around colorism are very "colorism is bad and people don't like dark skinned people"—and that's that! Nothing more is said and not enough non-dark skinned people especially in the environmental movement acknowledge it as a systemic issue. Dark-skin non-men are disproportionately left out of the outdoor space and this becomes even more of an issue when looking at it from an intersectional lens. Also, fatphobia, anti-Blackness, disability. —Celine, traditional home of the Haudenosaunee (Ho-deh-no-show-nee), Anishinaabe (Ah-nish-nah-bay), and Neutral People, otherwise known as Kitchener-Waterloo

☀ **GLOBAL WATER** quality and equity is not talked about enough. Sure, we hear a lot about the oceans, plastic waste, and oil spills, but there needs to be more of a focus on potable drinking water FOR ALL. So many people around the world trust their drinking water supplies and sewage systems but are being let down by their government officials and are being systemically forced into unfavorable conditions due to their race and socioeconomic status. Flint, Michigan, is still experiencing a water crisis and it seems to be widely overlooked at this point. Not to mention the hundreds of other communities within the United States and around the world that are experiencing unsafe WASH (water, sanitation, and hygiene) conditions. Water is life—without equal access to clean water, we have no life worth living. —Michelle, Philadelphia, PA

☀ **I THINK** one (of many) is the lack of clean drinking water and boil water advisories for indigenous communities in Canada. —Meghan Buck, Ontario, Canada

- ✳ **CHEMICALS OF** concern in material flows!!! Products like textiles and plastics are made with toxic chemicals that cause developmental harm in humans and they accumulate in the circular economy. The longer these harmful chemicals remain in products, the longer we are exposed to them and the more they build up in recycled materials! There are limits on chemical content in products so they eventually become waste and prevent a sustainable recycling process. Safe by design in the primary intervention to promote a sustainable circular economy and avoid harmful chemical exposures in humans!! —Maggie Hurley, Amherst, MA
- ✳ **THE FLINT** water crisis. —Elizondo, MI
- ✳ **ANIMAL AGRICULTURE.** —Saffron, Toronto, Ontario
- ✳ **POC IN** Asia, Africa, South America, Pacific Islands face disproportionate burden and ongoing impacts of colonialism. —Alexia, Austin, TX
- ✳ **THE GLOBAL** north sending recyclables to the global south. —Mia
- ✳ **THE INTERSECTION** of the climate crisis and disability. —Rebecca, Sheffield, UK
- ✳ **MINING COMPANIES** and the impact on sacred places in outback Australia. —Anonymous
- ✳ **COAL MINING** in Southern Appalachia. —Anonymous
- ✳ **PEOPLE IN** Eastern Indonesia are living side-by-side to extreme pollution, many die because of the ashes and air pollution around them. —Sharlene, Indonesia
- ✳ **THE GENTRIFICATION** of thrifting among youth. —Isa, Denmark
- ✳ **HIDDEN MASS** deforestation in the Appalachian. —Callie
- ✳ **THE INTERSECTION** of environmental and disability justice. —Celine, CA

157

* **THE WATER** crisis in Chile. —Annika, Maryland
* **NOISE POLLUTION,** communities near airports and other loud constant noise. —Anonymous
* **FAILING WASTEWATER** infrastructure in rural communities. —Ruby K., AL
* **HOW SUSTAINABILITY** is normal in Asia and within Indigenous cultures for centuries, but conversations on this topic are US/UK centered. —Ninoksha, Dubai
* **ENERGY JUSTICE.** —Kathryn, CA

WHY IS INTERSECTIONAL ENVIRONMENTALISM IMPORTANT AND/OR WHAT DOES IT MEAN TO YOU?

* **CONTEXT OF** approach must reflect the environment. —AJ, Bujumbura, Burundi
* **IT MEANS** real, just solutions, not just band-aid fixes. —Sara, Washington, DC
* **BECAUSE YOU** can't pull on one thread without making a knot somewhere else. —Shelby, MN
* **IF WE** want to truly make an impact, EVERYone needs to be able to do so. —Dani, @happy_dani
* **INTERSECTIONALITY SPOTLIGHTS** the nexus between health, inequity, and the environment. —Tan B., VA
* **IT IS** the only way out of this crisis. We need collective, global liberation. —Lia, Washington, DC
* **EQUAL ACCESS** to the outdoors and the world's natural resources. —Maddie, NJ
* **WITH IE** we can address the common roots of all the problems our society faces. —Katarina, Slovakia
* **PROVIDING A** better future for a generation that doesn't exist yet. —Jackie, San Francisco, CA

* **IT BRINGS** attention to the overall injustice in our world and how it is intertwined. —Anonymous

* **THE INTERSECTION** between environmental justice and reproductive justice: the ability for women to live in environments free of harmful toxins that could lead to reproductive health issues, the ability for children to grow up in a safe and healthy environment, and green spaces available for child rearing. And so much more! —Natalia, Waltham, MA

WHAT ADVICE WOULD YOU GIVE TO ENVIRONMENTALISTS WHO WANT TO TAKE ACTION?

* **DON'T LET** anyone (not even yourself) slow you down. Your passion can push you to great lengths and following your heart will take you farther than you could ever imagine. There will always be people who question your approach and who will belittle your ideas to amplify their own. As long as you are committed to the work and staying true to yourself, the rest will follow. You are capable of so much more than what others see. EVERYONE can make a difference and each idea can blossom into great change if it is nurtured appropriately. —Michelle, Philadelphia, PA

* **VOTE WITH** your dollar!! Support and promote companies and products that are transparent with their ingredient lists and are made safe by design! —Maggie, Hurley, Massachusetts

* **DON'T STOP** the fight. There will always be a moment or a person that will have different opinions than you and will try and fight you about it. Try to not engage because they want you to get angry so they can use your anger against you. —Andrea James, Atlanta, GA

* **NEVER GIVE** up. —Isabel, Austin, TX
* **JUST DO** it! We don't have time to put it off, be our earth's advocate. —Sasha, Los Angeles, CA
* **ASK YOURSELF,** what's my unique skill? Then combine that to create your unique mode of change. Acknowledge climate grief. Celebrate climate joy with your communities. Learn from the people around you, friends, mentors, and current changemakers. —Celine, Berkeley, CA
* **START SMALL;** don't be afraid to learn. —Sarah P.
* **WHEN YOU** show up for action, make sure everyone is represented. —Chanel R., Toronto, Ontario
* **FIND A** community! Find an organization that's doing what you're passionate about. —Anonymous
* **LISTEN TO** Indigenous people first. —Anonymous
* **TEACH PATIENCE** in the process. —Luke, MI
* **LOOK WITHIN** your own community. —Penelopi, Chicago, IL
* **JOIN AN** existing community and movement. —Alexia, Austin, TX
* **SUPPORT AND** amplify Indigenous-led environmental issues and organizations. —Emmaline, Brooklyn, NY

SOCIAL CHANGE 101: THE DEFINITIONS OF AND DISTINCTIONS AMONG "ACTIVIST," "ADVOCATE," AND "ORGANIZER"

THESE TERMS mean very different things to different people, especially as our world becomes more digital, but here's a brief breakdown of their definitions and distinctions.

✳ **ACTIVIST :** Someone who works to support a cause and campaigns for change. Activism consists of efforts to promote, impede, direct, or intervene in social, political, economic, or environmental reform with the desire to make changes in society toward a perceived greater good. Forms of activism vary and are often up for debate, but they can consist of demonstration (rallies, strikes, protests), petitioning, participating in a political campaign, artivism (using art), digital activism, economic activism (choosing to support mission-aligned brands), and more.

Historically, activists have also relied on literature (books, fliers, pamphlets, zines) to disseminate their message, and contemporary activist groups are utilizing social media in new ways to facilitate civic engagement and collective action combining politics with technology. The most highly visible and impactful activism often comes in the form of collective action, in which numerous individuals coordinate an act of protest together in order to make a bigger impact.

✳ **ADVOCATE :** Someone who fights for something or someone, especially someone who fights for the rights of others. Examples: A parent fighting for education services for their child, a lawyer who specializes in child protection and who speaks for abused children in court, a proponent of veganism who raises awareness about industrial agriculture. An advocate supports or argues for a cause, policy, framework, or way of living. Advocacy has many forms but largely uses education and awareness building. Many advocates also act as volunteers for the causes they support.

✳ **ORGANIZER :** Someone who works to create unity and solidarity and help their community members work together to solve problems and reach shared goals. An organizer can also be the person who organizes demonstrations, community events, and more. According to brightest.io, organizing is deeply rooted in community. Community organizing is a democratic strategy used by social movements, labor unions, underrepresented communities, and marginalized groups to gain rights, win collective political power, and create positive change. It requires long-term community investment.

INTERSECTIONAL ENVIRONMENTALISM 101

BELOW ARE some of my favorite books, articles, videos, and podcasts to help deepen your understanding of IE.

READ:

* *All We Can Save: Truth, Courage, and Solutions for the Climate Crisis,* edited by Ayana Elizabeth Johnson and Katharine K. Wilkinson
* *Black Faces, White Spaces: Reimagining the Relationship of African Americans to the Great Outdoors* by Carolyn Finney
* *Unequal Protection: Environmental Justice and Communities of Color,* edited by Robert D. Bullard
* *A Terrible Thing to Waste: Environmental Racism and Its Assault on the American Mind* by Harriet A. Washington
* *Youth to Power: Your Voice and How to Use It* by Jamie Margolin
* *Farming While Black: Soul Fire Farm's Practical Guide to Liberation on the Land* by Leah Penniman
* *Indigenous Environmental Justice,* edited by Karen Jarratt-Snider and Marianne O. Nielsen

* ***Environmental Justice in a Moment of Danger*** by Julie Sze
* ***Climate Change from the Streets: How Conflict and Collaboration Strengthen the Environmental Justice Movement*** by Michael Méndez
* ***Latinx Environmentalisms: Place, Justice, and the Decolonial,*** edited by Sarah D. Wald, David J. Vázquez, Priscilla Solis Ybarra, and Sarah Jaquette Ray
* ***Full Spectrum Resistance*** by Aric McBay
* ***Poisoned Water: How the Citizens of Flint, Michigan, Fought for Their Lives and Warned the Nation*** by Candy J. Cooper with Marc Aronson
* ***Clean and White: A History of Environmental Racism in the United States*** by Carl A. Zimring
* ***Race, Place, and Environmental Justice After Hurricane Katrina: Struggles to Reclaim, Rebuild, and Revitalize New Orleans and the Gulf Coast,*** edited by Robert D. Bullard and Beverly Wright
* ***Waste: One Woman's Fight Against America's Dirty Secret*** by Catherine Coleman Flowers
* ***Cultivating Food Justice: Race, Class, and Sustainability,*** edited by Alison Hope Alkon and Julian Agyeman

WATCH:

* ***Environmental Justice, Explained*** (Grist)
* ***Rise: Standing Rock,*** parts one and two (Vice)
* ***A Brief History of Environmental Justice*** (ProPublica)
* ***Environmental Justice: Peggy Shepard*** (TEDxHarlem)
* ***Environmental Racism Is the New Jim Crow*** (The Atlantic)
* ***Come Hell or High Water: The Battle for Turkey Creek*** (PBS)
* ***Beyond Recognition*** (Kanopy)

- *Urban Roots* (Tree Media)
- *An American Ascent* (Sundance Now)
- *What Is Environmental Racism?* (AJ+)
- *"Man-Killing Jobs" and Environmental Racism* (The Atlantic)
- *Colour of Pollution: Environmental Racism* (The Stream)
- *Oil, Gas, and the Effects of Environmental Racism* (Vice TV)
- *What Is Environmental Racism?* (Climate in Colour)
- *What It's Like to Live in Cancer Alley* (NowThis)
- *That's Fracked: Can a Colorado School Combat Environmental Racism?* (The Daily Show)

LISTEN (PODCASTS):

- *How to Save a Planet* with Dr. Ayana Elizabeth Johnson and Alex Blumberg
- *Yikes* with Mikaela Loach and Jo Becker
- *Conscious Chatter* with Kestrel Jenkins, episode 102: "Melanin and Sustainable Style + Ethical Fashion as a Privileged White Girl Thing"
- *Dismantled* by Intersectional Environmentalist
- *Drilled* with Amy Westervelt
- *Green Dreamer* with Kamea Chayne
- *Living Downstream* by KRCB-FM
- *Hot Take* with Amy Westervelt and Mary Annaïse Heglar
- *For the Moment,* episode: "Environmental Racism: It's a Thing" by Stitcher

VERNICE'S RECOMMENDED READING LIST FOR INTERSECTIONAL ENVIRONMENTALISTS

A CURATED list of resources from environmental justice pioneer Vernice Miller-Travis.

REPORTS:

✳ "Toxic Wastes and Race in the United States: A National Report on the Racial and Socio-Economic Characteristics of Communities with Hazardous Waste Sites," Commission for Racial Justice, United Church of Christ, 1987

✳ Proceedings: "The First National People of Color Environmental Leadership Summit," United Church of Christ, Commission for Racial Justice, 1992

✳ "Symposium on Health Research and Needs to Ensure Environmental Justice," sponsored by U.S. HHS: National Institute of Environmental Health Sciences, NIH Office of Minority Health, U.S. EPA, NIOSH, CDC, ATSDR, U.S. DOE, CDC National Center for Environmental Health, August 1994

BOOKS:

✳ *Streets of Hope: The Fall and Rise of an Urban Neighborhood* by Peter Medoff and Holly Sklar (South End Press, 1994): The story of the groundbreaking work of the Dudley Street Neighborhood Initiative in the Roxbury community of Boston, Massachusetts

✳ *All Our Relations: Native Struggles for Land and Life* by Winona LaDuke (South End Press, 1999)

* ***Latino Metropolis*** by Victor M. Valle and Rodolfo D. Torres (University of Minnesota Press, 2000)

* ***Sprawl City: Race, Politics, and Planning in Atlanta,*** edited by Robert D. Bullard, Glenn S. Johnson, and Angel O. Torres (Island Press, 2000)

* ***American Project: The Rise and Fall of a Modern Ghetto*** by Sudhir Alladi Venkatesh (Harvard University Press, 2000)

* ***Root Shock: How Tearing Up City Neighborhoods Hurts America, and What We Can Do About It*** by Mindy Thompson Fullilove, MD (A One World/Ballantine Book, 2004)

* ***The Quest for Environmental Justice: Human Rights and the Politics of Pollution,*** edited by Robert D. Bullard (Sierra Club Books, 2005)

* ***The Environment and the People in American Cities, 1600s–1900s: Disorder, Inequality, and Social Change*** by Dorceta E. Taylor (Duke University Press, 2009)

* ***The Rise of the American Conservation Movement: Power, Privilege, and Environmental Protection*** by Dorceta E. Taylor (Duke University Press, 2016)

RESOURCES BY CATEGORY

FROM THE intersectionalenvironmentalist.com resource hub. Each list of recommendations was compiled by an intersectional environmentalist and IE topic leader. To dive deeper into each resource page, visit inter sectionalenvironmentalist.com, and I encourage you to check out the incredible work of each inspiring topic leader.

AGRICULTURE

CURATED BY Amber Tamm

BOOKS AND ARTICLES:

* ✳ "Innovations by Black farmers remain at the core of sustainable agriculture today": *Mother Jones*, "White People Own 98 Percent of Rural Land. Young Black Farmers Want to Reclaim Their Share" by Tom Philpott
* ✳ "Carrying on the legacy of our ancestral grandmothers, who braided seeds in their hair before boarding transatlantic slave ships, believing against odds in a future of sovereignty on land": *Farming While Black: Soul Fire Farm's Practical Guide to Liberation on the Land* by Leah Penniman
* ✳ "While this article is practical in nature, it is also full of some of my most sacred friends and relatives—the plant nations who give their lives to nourish, protect, and heal us. As we

sit in quarantine, I would like for you to think about your traditional foods and make a promise that you will get out and collect them in a good way, following the protocols put in place by your predecessors": "Hope in the Time of Stress" by Linda Black Elk

✳ A food column on Medium dedicated to exploring recipes and food justice and to dismantling systems of oppression in agriculture: Heated by Medium x Mark Bittman

✳ George Washington Carver, a prominent Black scientist in the early twentieth century, was an American agricultural scientist and inventor. He was known for preventing soil depletion through alternative ag methods: "A Curation of George Washington Carver Publications" by Mason Trappio

✳ "Addressing systemic racism in U.S. agriculture has to begin with the USDA": op-ed: "The Farm Bureau Says It Wants to Fight Racism. Here's Where to Start" by John Boyd and Scott Faber

✳ "The first edition of *Gaia's Garden* sparked the imagination of America's home gardeners, introducing permaculture's central message: working with Nature, not against her, results in more beautiful, abundant, and forgiving gardens": *Gaia's Garden: A Guide to Home-Scale Permaculture*, second edition, by Toby Hemenway

✳ "Michael Carter Jr.—Carter Farms is a century farm in the Piedmont region of Virginia that specializes in growing ethnic, African tropical vegetables organically. Michael is the only other person that we know that has grown on the continent, Afrika, and back here": *Jigìjìgì: Africulture* podcast featuring Michael Carter Jr. by Mason Olonade

✳ "Part memoir, nutritional primer, and political manifesto, this controversial examination exposes the destructive history of agriculture—causing the devastation of prairies and forests, driving countless species extinct, altering the climate, and destroying the topsoil—and asserts that, in order to save the planet, food must come from within living communities": *The Vegetarian Myth: Food, Justice, and Sustainability* by Lierre Keith

ORGANIZATIONS TO SUPPORT:

* **A GROWING CULTURE**
* **UNIVERSE CITY NYC**
* **NORTHEAST FARMERS OF COLOR LAND TRUST**
* **BLACK FARMER FUND**
* **THE NATIVE AMERICAN FOOD SOVEREIGNTY ALLIANCE**
* **BLACK PERMACULTURE NETWORK**
* **THE NATIONAL YOUNG FARMERS COALITION**

OCEANS

RESOURCES CURATED by Inka Cresswell,
with support from Lonely Whale

READ:

* "We need to empower coastal communities for sustainable fisheries, because they are the guardians of the ocean—we need to value their traditional knowledge": "Guardians of the Ocean" by Vatosoa Rakotondrazafy
* "Currently, there are few people of color and people from developing nations in the deep-sea sphere. That needs to change if leaders want to truly say they are having a 'global conversation'": "My Deep Sea, My Backyard: Empowering

Nations to Study the Deep" by Melissa Cristina Márquez

✳ "Seventy percent of our coastlines are in the developing world, but representation at the global stage is disproportional. The harsh truth is, if we aren't being inclusive and equitable, we aren't going to move the needle on the things that really matter, the things that are integral to our very existence, and we will continue to fail…So, if we truly want to save our oceans, never forget: every coastline needs a local hero": "The Problem of 'Colonial Science'" by Asha de Vos

✳ "Ocean justice is where ocean conservation and social justice intersect. If we think about where is the water the most polluted, who gets impacted by storms, who is most dependent on the ocean and suffers when there's overfishing, it often is poor communities and communities of color along the coastline. When we think about ocean conservation, it can't just be for the spots in front of fancy resorts or the homes of wealthy individuals. We should also be thinking about not just who bears the brunt of the impacts on the ocean, but who gets the benefit when we do take care of it." —Ayana Elizabeth Johnson, "Ocean Justice: Where Social Equity and the Climate Fight Intersect," an interview with Dr. Ayana Elizabeth Johnson by Beth Gardiner

✳ This article explains different Indigenous fishing systems that are much more sustainable and emphasizes how they are "centered on a reciprocal relationship with the environment in which harvesters are also salmon stewards": "Want to Save B.C. Salmon? Bring Back Indigenous Fishing Systems, Study Says," by Stephanie Wood

✳ Wealthy countries had grown accustomed to exporting their plastic problems, with little thought or effort to ensure that the plastic they were exporting got recycled and did not harm other countries. North Americans and Europeans exported not just their plastic waste, but the pollution that went with getting rid of it...Last year China enacted a new policy, called National Sword, for economic and environmental reasons including pollution from importing and processing plastic waste. By refusing to be the world's dumping ground, China's policy—and the fallout that resulted from it—revealed the true cost of rampant consumption, plastic production, and the problems and limitations of recycling as a solution to a world suffocating in its own plastic: "Discarded: Communities on the Frontlines of the Global Plastic Crisis" by Global Alliance for Incinerator Alternatives (GAIA)

WATCH:

MY 25: THE OCEAN BETWEEN US

My 25: The Ocean Between Us is an authored short film switching between memories and reality to tell an intimate story of how our oceans have changed from the perspective of multiple generations exploring the state of our oceans and ultimately their fate.

KOKOLY

Against a backdrop of climate breakdown, personal loss, and a marine environment changing beyond her control, Kokoly lives on a knife edge. This is her story. #FishingForSurvival.

DIVING WITH A PURPOSE: THE SLAVE WRECKS PROJECT BY NATIONAL GEOGRAPHIC EXPLORER TARA ROBERTS

Led by African American archival researchers, marine archaeologists, and expert scuba divers, the team at *Diving with a Purpose* connects maritime archaeology with conservation to tell the stories of their ancestors.

LISTEN:

✳ "Black Lives Matter in Ocean Conservation with Danni Washington," *Speak Up for the Ocean Blue* (podcast)

✳ *52 Hertz*, a Lonely Whale podcast, episode two: Steff McDermott: Steff McDermott (@TheAmazingSteff_) shared more about her environmental journey in a new series, *Sail for Climate Action,* with fellow youth activists working for a more just, equitable future

✳ Amanda Gorman's "Ode to Our Ocean," written in collaboration with Atmos, Future Earth, and Lonely Whale

ACTIVIST AND NONPROFIT ORGANIZATIONS TO SUPPORT:

✳ **BLUE VENTURES**
  ✳ https://explore.blueventures.org/building-resilience
  ✳ "Blue Ventures develops transformative approaches for catalyzing and sustaining locally led marine conservation. We work in places where the ocean is vital to local cultures and economies, and are committed to protecting marine biodiversity in ways that benefit coastal people."

✳ MISS ELASMO

- ✳ https://www.misselasmo.org
- ✳ "We strive to be seen and take up space in a discipline which has been largely inaccessible for women like us. We strive to be positive role models for the next generation. We seek to promote diversity and inclusion in shark science and encourage women of color to push through barriers and contribute knowledge in marine science."

✳ FISH 'N FINS (Caribbean)

- ✳ https://www.aquafishnfins.com
- ✳ "Fish 'N Fins is...[a] nonprofit kids' ocean club which teaches local children to swim, snorkel, and dive in a fun and safe environment, focused on learning about the ocean and how we can play a key part in the long-term protection of our oceans."

✳ OCEANSWELL (BIPOC owned)

- ✳ https://www.instagram.com/oceanswellorg/
- ✳ https://blogs.scientificamerican.com/observations/9-ocean -conservation-groups-you-dont-know-about-but-should/
- ✳ Sri Lanka's first marine conservation research and education organization, focused on "educating the next generation of diverse ocean heroes, equipping students from underrepresented nations to conduct marine conservation research."

✳ ALLIGATOR HEAD FOUNDATION

- ✳ https://www.alligatorheadfoundation.org
- ✳ "We work for fish-filled seas, abundant reefs, and thriving communities."

✳ BLACK GIRLS DIVE FOUNDATION
  - ✳ https://www.blackgirlsdivefoundation.org/our-adventures
  - ✳ "We provide opportunities for young girls and women to experience life in the water through outreach, scholarships, and education."

✳ BYE BYE PLASTIC BAGS
  - ✳ http://www.byebyeplasticbags.org/
  - ✳ "A movement powered by youth around the world to say NO to plastic bags."

✳ RISE ST. JAMES
  - ✳ https://www.rollingstone.com/politics/politics -features/louisiana-cancer-alley-getting-more -toxic-905534/
  - ✳ https://www.stopformosa.org/
  - ✳ "Formosa Plastics wants to build a massive plastic factory on the banks of the Mississippi River in St. James, Louisiana…This African American community has already been sickened by industrial polluters. The region is referred to as 'Cancer Alley' or 'Death Alley' by those who live and die there and a new plastic plant will pose greater risk to public health…Louisiana is permitting Formosa to discharge toxic chemicals into the air and water, including New Orleans's water supply…It's part of the fossil fuel industry's push to turn an oversupply of fracked natural gas into more throwaway plastic. Plastic that may choke wildlife and add to the ocean plastic crisis…We can't let that happen."

DISCOVER OVER fifteen topic pages on intersectionalenvironmentalist. com and via Instagram @intersectionalenvironmentalist.

ACKNOWLEDGMENTS

I'D LIKE to send my thanks to my mom, dad, and sister—Jazell, Cameron, and Camara—and my grandparents, Janice, Jerry, Joyce, and Dorthy, who always encouraged me to follow my dreams.

To Jesse, Tyler, Karina, Illysa, Olivia, Abby, Drew, Kim, Nisa, and Anjola—who have nourished me with the most beautiful friendships.

To Laura Lee Mattingly at Present Perfect Lit and Emma and Thea at Voracious, who believed in my writing.

To my team at Little, Brown: Lauren Ortiz, Jessica Chun, Ben Allen, Nyamekye Waliyaya, and Kirin Diemont.

To Alexa Terfloth for showing me design is a powerful vehicle for change.

To Marissa, Julia, and Sydnie at Team Aire for helping me spread my wings.

To Dr. Keller for encouraging me to go to Kansas and start my environmental journey.

To all the contributors to this book, for helping demonstrate the power of coalition building, accountability, and collaboration.

To all the environmental justice elders and frontline activists and advocates. This book would not exist without the foundations they laid and the work they continue to do.

To Kimberlé Williams Crenshaw, the Combahee River Collective, and Audre Lorde for your lessons on intersectionality and the beauty of Black girl magic. This book would not be possible without you.

NOTES

CHAPTER 1

[1] Smithsonian Channel. "Malcolm X's Fiery Speech Addressing Police Brutality." February 16, 2018. YouTube video, 02:48. https://www.youtube.com/watch?v=6_uYWDyYNUg.

[2] Burkett, Elinor. "Women's Rights Movement." *Encyclopedia Britannica*. Last modified on November 6, 2020. https://www.britannica.com/event/womens-movement.

[3] Brunell, Laura, and Burkett, Elinor. "Feminism." *Encyclopedia Britannica*. Last modified on March 24, 2021. https://www.britannica.com/topic/feminism.

[4] Muhammad, A.J. "Black Feminism Introductory Research Guide." *The New York Public Library*. Last modified on February 5, 2020. https://www.nypl.org/blog/2018/06/29/black-feminism-introductory-research-guide.

[5] Bailey, Moya, and Trudy. "On Misogynoir: Citation, Erasure, and Plagiarism," *Feminist Media Studies*, no. 18.4 (2018): 762–768, doi: 10.1080/14680777.2018.1447395.

[6] Masequesmay, Gina. "Sexism." *Encyclopedia Britannica*. Last modified on May 28, 2020. https://www.britannica.com/topic/sexism.

[7] Rabin, Roni Caryn. "Huge Racial Disparities Found in Deaths Linked to Pregnancy." *The New York Times*. Last modified on May 7, 2019. https://www.nytimes.com/2019/05/07/health/pregnancy-deaths-.html.

[8] Davis, Angela. *Freedom Is a Constant Struggle*. Edited by Frank Barat. Chicago, IL: Haymarket Books, 2015.

[9] Combahee River Collective, The. "The Combahee River Collective Statement." 1977. Accessed May 21, 2021. https://americanstudies.yale .edu/sites/default/files/files/Keyword%20Coalition_Readings.pdf.

10 Taylor, Keeanga-Yamahtta. "Until Black Women Are Free, None of Us Will Be Free: Barbara Smith and the Black Feminist Visionaries of the Combahee River Collective." *The New Yorker.* Last modified on July 20, 2020. https://www.newyorker.com /news/our-columnists/until-black-women-are-free-none-of-us -will-be-free.

11 Ibid.

12 Ibid.

13 Lang, Cady. "President Trump Has Attacked Critical Race Theory. Here's What to Know About the Intellectual Movement." *Time.* Last modified on September 29, 2020. https://time .com/5891138/critical-race-theory-explained/.

14 Merriam-Webster.com dictionary, sv "intersectionality," accessed June 11, 2021, https://www.merriam-webster.com/dictionary/intersec tionality.

15 Coaston, Jane. "The Intersectionality Wars." Vox. Last modified on May 28, 2019. https://www.vox.com/the-highlight/2019/5/20 /18542013/intersectionality-conservatism-law-race-gender -discrimination.

16 Ibid.

17 Murphy, Andye. "Greeting Goddess Gaia." *Gaia.* Last modified on April 13, 2016. https://www.gaia.com/article/goddess-gaia.

18 Gabrielle. "Seven Other Names for Mother Earth." *Shamans Market.* Last modified on April 23, 2018. http://blog.shamansmarket .com/seven-other-names-for-mother-earth/.

19 Miles, Kathryn. "Ecofeminism: Sociology and Environmentalism." *Ency-clopedia Britannica.* Last modified on October 9, 2018. https:// www.britannica.com/topic/ecofeminism.

20 Mills, Patricia Jagentowicz. "Feminism and Ecology: On the Domina-tion of Nature." *Hypatia*, no. 6.1 (1991): 162–78. http://www.jstor .org/stable/3810039.

21 Petruzzello, Melissa. "Chipko Movement." *Encyclopedia Britannica.* Last modified on May 24, 2021. https://www.britannica.com /topic/Chipko-movement.

22 Miles, "Ecofeminism."

23 Ibid.

24 Last, Angela. "Shiva, Vandana." *Global Social Theory.* Accessed May 21, 2021. https://globalsocialtheory.org/thinkers/shiva -vandana/.

CHAPTER 2

[1] "Environmental Justice Timeline." *United States Environmental Protection Agency.* Accessed May 21, 2021. https://www.epa.gov/environmentaljustice/environmental-justice-timeline.

[2] Ibid.

[3] Hautzinger, Daniel. "The Chicago Woman Who Fought to Clean Up the Southeast Side." *WTTW.* Last modified on February 24, 2020. https://interactive.wttw.com/playlist/2020/02/24/hazel-johnson.

[4] Ibid.

[5] "Historical Hero of the Week: Hazel M. Johnson." *Our Daily Planet.* Last modified on February 12, 2021. https://www.ourdailyplanet.com/story/historical-hero-of-the-week-hazel-m-johnson/.

[6] Hautzinger, "The Chicago Woman."

[7] Ibid.

[8] Ibid.

[9] "The Principles of Environmental Justice (EJ)." *NRDC.* Last modified on December 15, 2016. https://www.nrdc.org/resources/principles-environmental-justice-ej.

[10] Agbor, Phylisha W. "Robert Doyle Bullard (1946–)." BlackPast.org. Last modified on December 24, 2017. https://www.blackpast.org/african-american-history/bullard-dr-robert-doyle-1946/.

[11] Ibid.

[12] Apeel team. "The History of Black Excellence in Social Justice: Dr. Robert Bullard." *Apeel* blog. Last modified on February 19, 2021. https://blog.apeelsciences.com/dr-robert-bullard.

[13] Dicum, Gregory. "Meet Robert Bullard, the Father of Environmental Justice." *Grist.* Last modified on March 15, 2006. https://grist.org/article/dicum/.

[14] "Bean v. Southwestern Waste Management Corp.: Significance, Waste Management in Houston, Laches and State Action, Impact, Further Readings." *Law Library—American Law and Legal Information.* Accessed June 1, 2021. https://law.jrank.org/pages/13187/Bean-v-Southwestern-Waste-Management-Corp.html.

[15] Bullard, Robert. "Environmental Justice for All." *Nature Transformed, TeacherServe®. National Humanities Center.* Accessed May 21, 2021. http://nationalhumanitiescenter.org/tserve/nattrans/ntuseland/essays/envjust.htm.

[16] Ibid.

[17] "Environmental Justice Timeline."

[18] Lapin, Nicole, and Jason Hanna. "1969 Alcatraz Takeover 'Changed the Whole Course of History.'" *CNN*. Last modified on November 20, 2009. https://www.cnn.com/2009/CRIME/11/20/alcatraz .indian.occupation/.

[19] Ibid.

[20] Latson, Jennifer. "The Burning River That Sparked a Revolution." *Time*. Last modified on June 22, 2015. https://time.com/3921976 /cuyahoga-fire/.

[21] Ibid.

[22] "The History of Earth Day." *Earth Day*. Accessed June 13, 2021. https://www.earthday.org/history/.

[23] Mangan, Arty. "Earth Day, White Privilege and Decolonizing the Mind." *Bioneers*. Accessed May 21, 2021. https://bioneers.org /earth-day-white-privilege-decolonizing-the-mind-zmbz2004/.

[24] Ibid.

[25] Ibid.

[26] Gardiner, Beth. "This Landmark Law Saved Millions of Lives and Trillions of Dollars." *National Geographic*. Last modified on May 4, 2021. https://www.nationalgeographic.com/environment/article/clean-air -act-saved-millions-of-lives-trillions-of-dollars.

[27] Beinhorn, Klara. "Environmental Justice Movement as a History." Accessed May 21, 2021. https://scalar.usc.edu/works/petro leum-refineries-and-the-future/environmental-justice-move ment-as-a-history.

[28] Ibid.

[29] "Siting of Hazardous Waste Landfills and Their Correlation with Racial and Economic Status of Surrounding Communities." U.S. Government Accountability Office. Last modified on June 14, 1983. https://www.gao.gov/products/rced-83-168.

[30] Schlanger, Zoë. "Race Is the Biggest Indicator in the US of Whether You Live Near Toxic Waste." *Quartz*. Last modified on March 22, 2017. https://qz.com/939612/race-is-the-biggest-indicator-in -the-us-of-whether-you-live-near-toxic-waste/.

CHAPTER 3

[1] Chandler, Leigh. "Your Full Self: Social Identities and the Workplace." *YW Boston*. Last modified on October 27, 2020. https://www

.ywboston.org/2020/10/your-full-self-social-identities-and-the
-workplace/.

2 Merriam-Webster.com dictionary, sv "social construct," accessed
June 11, 2021, https://www.merriam-webster.com/dictionary
/social%20construct.

3 Du Bois, W.E.B. (William Edward Burghardt). *Black Reconstruction in
America: An Essay Toward a History of the Part Which Black Folk
Played in the Attempt to Reconstruct Democracy in America,
1860–1880.* Oxford: Oxford University Press, 2007.

4 Ibid.

5 Ibid.

6 McIntosh, Peggy. "White Privilege and Male Privilege: A Personal
Account of Coming to See Correspondences Through Work in
Women's Studies." In *Race, Class, and Gender: An Anthology,*
edited by Margaret L. Andersen and Patricia Hill Collins, 76–87.
Belmont, CA: Wadsworth, 1988.

7 Lu, Denise; Jon Huang; Ashwin Seshagiri; Haeyoun Park; and Troy
Griggs. "Faces of Power: 80% Are White, Even as U.S. Becomes
More Diverse." *The New York Times.* Last modified on
September 10, 2020. https://www.nytimes.com/interactive
/2020/09/09/us/powerful-people-race-us.html.

8 Ibid.

9 Henderson, Nia-Malika. "White Men Are 31 Percent of the American
Population. They Hold 65 Percent of All Elected Offices." *The
Washington Post.* Last modified on April 26, 2019. https://www
.washingtonpost.com/news/the-fix/wp/2014/10/08/65-percent
-of-all-american-elected-officials-are-white-men/.

10 Statista Research Department. "U.S. Population by Gender
2010–2024." *Statista.* Last modified on May 11, 2021. https://
www.statista.com/statistics/737923/us-population-by-gender/.

11 Sáenz, Rogelio, and Dudley L. Poston. "Children of Color Projected
to Be Majority of U.S. Youth This Year." *PBS.* Last modified on
January 9, 2020. https://www.pbs.org/newshour/nation/children
-of-color-projected-to-be-majority-of-u-s-youth-this-year.

12 Gal, Shayanne; Andy Kiersz; Michelle Mark; Ruobing Su; and Margue-
rite Ward. "26 Simple Charts to Show Friends and Family Who
Aren't Convinced Racism Is Still a Problem in America." *Business
Insider.* Last modified on July 8, 2020. https://www.businessinsi
der.com/us-systemic-racism-in-charts-graphs-data-2020-6.

[13] Matthews, Dylan. "The Massive New Study on Race and Economic Mobility in America, Explained." Vox. Last modified on March 21, 2018. https://www.vox.com/policy-and-politics/2018/3/21/17139300/economic-mobility-study-race-black-white-women-men-incarceration-income-chetty-hendren-jones-porter.

[14] Ibid.

[15] "Nonwhite School Districts Get $23 Billion Less than White Districts." EdBuild. Accessed June 11, 2021. https://edbuild.org/content/23-billion.

[16] Jones, Charisse. "Race Matters: Gap between Black and White Home-ownership Is Vast, New Report Finds." *USA Today*. Last modified on June 29, 2020. https://www.usatoday.com/story/money/2020/06/29/black-homeownership-lags-whites-fueling-wealth-gap-report-finds/3244738001/.

[17] "Report to the United Nations on Racial Disparities in the U.S. Criminal Justice System." *The Sentencing Project*. Last modified on May 1, 2018. https://www.sentencingproject.org/publications/un-report-on-racial-disparities/.

[18] Ibid.

[19] Seelye, John. "Who Was Horatio? The Alger Myth and American Scholarship." *American Quarterly* no. 4.17 (1965): 749–56, doi: 10.2307/2711132.

[20] Rice, Doyle. "Study Finds a Race Gap in Air Pollution—Whites Largely Cause It; Blacks and Hispanics Breathe It." *USA Today*. Last modified on March 12, 2019. https://www.usatoday.com/story/news/nation/2019/03/11/air-pollution-inequality-minorities-breathe-air-polluted-whites/3130783002/.

[21] Ibid.

[22] Cox, Bartees. "Environmental Racism Has Left Black Americans Three Times More Likely to Die from Pollution." *Quartz*. Last modified on March 13, 2018. https://qz.com/1226984/environmental-racism-has-left-black-americans-three-times-more-likely-to-die-from-pollution/.

[23] Ibid.

[24] Ruckart, Perri Zeitz; Adrienne S. Ettinger; Mona Hanna-Attisha; Nicole Jones; Stephanie I. Davis; and Patrick N. Breysse. "The Flint Water Crisis: A Coordinated Public Health Emergency Response and Recovery Initiative." *Journal of Public Health Management*

and Practice no. 25.1 (2019): S84–S90, doi: 10.1097/PHH.00 00000000000871.

[25] Ibid.

[26] Thomas, Leah. "Why Every Environmentalist Should Be Anti-Racist." *Vogue.* Last modified on October 27, 2020. https://www.vogue .com/article/why-every-environmentalist-should-be-anti-racist.

[27] Pastor, Manuel; Robert Bullard; James K. Boyce; Alice Fothergill; Rachel Morello-Frosch; and Beverly Wright. "Environment, Disaster, and Race After Katrina." *Race, Poverty & the Environment* no. 13.1 (2006): 21–26.

[28] Ibid.

[29] Ibid.

[30] Ibid.

[31] Ibid.

[32] Brooks, David. "The Storm After the Storm." *New York Times.* Last modified on September 1, 2005. https://www.nytimes.com/ 2005/09/01/opinion/the-storm-after-the-storm.html.

[33] Cooper, Dara. "What Is Food Justice?" *Dara Cooper.* Last modified on March 30, 2017. http://www.daracooper.com/food-justice-blog --more/what-is-food-justice.

CHAPTER 4

[1] Rudolph, Linda; Catherine Harrison; Laura Buckley; and Savannah North. *Climate Change, Health, and Equity: A Guide for Local Health Departments.* Oakland, CA, and Washington, DC., Public Health Institute and American Public Health Association, 2018. https://www.apha.org/-/media/files/pdf/topics/climate/climate _health_equity.ashx.

[2] Vespa, Jonathan; Lauren Medina; and David M. Armstrong. "Demographic Turning Points for the United States: Population Projections for 2020 to 2060." *Current Population Reports, P25-1144, U.S. Census Bureau.* Washington, DC, 2020. Accessed on May 21, 2021. https://www.census.gov/content/dam/Census /library/publications/2020/demo/p25-1144.pdf.

[3] "Black Population by State 2021." *World Population Review.* 21. Accessed June 13, 2021. https://worldpopulationreview.com /state-rankings/black-population-by-state.

[4] Vespa, "Demographic Turning Points."

[5] Gates, Henry Louis, Jr. "How Many Slaves Landed in the U.S.?" *The African Americans: Many Rivers to Cross with Henry Louis Gates Jr.* Accessed May 21, 2021. https://www.pbs.org/wnet/african -americans-many-rivers-to-cross/history/how-many-slaves -landed-in-the-us/.

[6] Rudolph, *Climate Change.*

[7] Ibid.

[8] Urofsky, Melvin I. "Jim Crow Law." *Encyclopedia Britannica.* Last modi- fied on February 12, 2021. https://www.britannica.com/event /Jim-Crow-law.

[9] Rudolph, *Climate Change.*

[10] "Fair Housing Act." *Federal Fair Lending Regulations and Statutes.* Accessed May 21, 2021. https://www.federalreserve.gov/board docs/supmanual/cch/fair_lend_fhact.pdf.

[11] Hoerner, J. Andrew, and Nia Robinson. "Just Climate Policy—Just Racial Policy." *Race, Poverty & the Environment* no. 16.2 (2009): 32–35.

[12] Hoerner, J. Andrew, and Nia Robinson, "A Climate of Change: African Americans, Global Warming, and a Just Climate Policy for the U.S." *Environmental Justice and Climate Change Initiative 2008.* Accessed May 21, 2021. http://urbanhabitat.org/files/climateof change.pdf.

[13] Ibid.

[14] Ibid.

[15] Ibid.

[16] Rudolph, *Climate Change.*

[17] Lakhani, Nina. "'Heat Islands': Racist Housing Policies in US Linked to Deadly Heatwave Exposure." *The Guardian.* Last modified on January 13, 2020. https://www.theguardian.com/society/2020 /jan/13/racist-housing-policies-us-deadly-heatwaves-exposure -study.

[18] Rudolph, *Climate Change.*

[19] Ibid.

[20] "Hispanic or Latino Origin." *U.S. Census Bureau, Population Estimates Program (PEP).* Accessed May 21, 2021. https://www.census.gov /quickfacts/fact/note/US/RHI725219#:~:text=for%20racial%20 categories.-,Definition,%E2%80%A2Puerto%20Rican.

[21] Ibid.

[22] Vespa, "Demographic Turning Points."

[23] Rudolph, *Climate Change.*

[24] Krogstad, Jens Manuel. "Hispanics Have Accounted for More than Half of Total U.S. Population Growth Since 2010." Pew Research Center. Last modified on July 10, 2020. https://www.pewresearch .org/fact-tank/2020/07/10/hispanics-have-accounted-for-more -than-half-of-total-u-s-population-growth-since-2010/.

[25] Ibid.

[26] Gregory, James. "Latinx Great Migrations—History and Geography." *America's Great Migrations Project.* Accessed June 13, 2021. https://depts.washington.edu/moving1/latinx_migration .shtml.

[27] Heidler, Jeanne T., and David S. Heidler. "Manifest Destiny." *Encyclopedia Britannica.* Last modified on April 2, 2021. https://www .britannica.com/event/Manifest-Destiny.

[28] Gregory, "Latinx Great Migrations."

[29] Ibid.

[30] Ibid.

[31] Rudolph, *Climate Change.*

[32] Ibid.

[33] Ibid.

[34] Ibid.

[35] Quintero, Adrianna; Valerie Jaffee; Jorge Madrid; Elsa Ramirez; and Andrea Delgado. "U.S. Latinos and Air Pollution: A Call to Action." *The National Wildlife Federation.* Last modified on September 28, 2011. Accessed June 13, 2021. https://www.nwf .org/Educational-Resources/Reports/2011/09-28-2011-US -Latinos-Air-Pollution.

[36] Rudolph, *Climate Change.*

[37] Reichmuth, David. "Inequitable Exposure to Air Pollution from Vehicles in California." *Union of Concerned Scientists.* Last modified on January 28, 2019. https://www.ucsusa.org/resources/inequitable -exposure-air-pollution-vehicles-california-2019.

[38] "Definitions of Food Security." *Economic Research Service, U.S. Department of Agriculture.* Last modified on September 9, 2020. https://www.ers.usda.gov/topics/food-nutrition-assistance/food -security-in-the-us/definitions-of-food-security.aspx.

[39] Gross, Liza. "Fields of Toxic Pesticides Surround the Schools of Ventura County—Are They Poisoning the Students?" *The Nation.* Last

modified on August 18, 2017. https://www.thenation.com/article
/archive/fields-toxic-pesticides-surround-schools-ventura-county
-are-they-poisoning-students/.

40 Norris, Tina; Paula L. Vines; and Elizabeth M. Hoeffel. "The American Indian and Alaska Native Population: 2010." *United States Census Bureau,* January 2012. https://www.census.gov/history/pdf/c2010br-10.pdf.

41 Ibid.

42 "Indian Country Demographics." *National Congress of American Indians.* Last modified on June 1, 2020. https://www.ncai.org/about-tribes/demographics.

43 Woodward, Aylin. "European Colonizers Killed So Many Indigenous Americans That the Planet Cooled Down, a Group of Researchers Concluded." *Insider.* Last modified on February 9, 2019. https://www.businessinsider.com/climate-changed-after-euro peans-killed-indigenous-americans-2019-2.

44 "Indian Country Demographics."

45 Ibid.

46 Rudolph, *Climate Change.*

47 Ibid.

48 Calma, Justine. "The Navajo Nation Faced Water Shortages for Generations—and Then the Pandemic Hit: No Running Water Is Making It Harder to Fight COVID-19." *The Verge.* Last modified on July 6, 2020. https://www.theverge.com/2020/7/6/21311211/navajo-nation-covid-19-running-water-access.

49 Rudolph, *Climate Change.*

50 Morales, Laurel. "Many Native Americans Can't Get Clean Water, Report Finds." *NPR.* Last modified on November 18, 2019. https://www.npr.org/2019/11/18/779821510/many-native-americans-cant-get-clean-water-report-finds.

51 Budiman, Abby, and Neil G. Ruiz. "Key Facts About Asian Americans, a Diverse and Growing Population." Pew Research Center. Last modified on April 29, 2021. https://www.pewresearch.org/fact -tank/2021/04/29/key-facts-about-asian-americans/.

52 Ibid.

53 "Race—Quick Facts." *United States Census Bureau.* Accessed June 1, 2021. https://www.census.gov/quickfacts/fact/note/US /RHI625219.

[54] Budiman, "Key Facts."

[55] Hixson, Lindsay; Bradford B. Hepler; and Myoung Ouk Kim. "The Native Hawaiian and Other Pacific Islander Population: 2010." *United States Census Bureau*. May 2012. https://www.census .gov/prod/cen2010/briefs/c2010br-12.pdf.

[56] "Native Hawaiians/Pacific Islanders." *U.S. Department of Health and Human Services*. Accessed June 14, 2021. https://minorityhealth .hhs.gov/omh/browse.aspx.

[57] Ibid.

[58] Hatcher, Nicholas L. "A Brief Timeline of Anti-Asian Discrimination in the U.S." *Teen Vogue*. Last modified on May 10, 2021. https:// www.teenvogue.com/story/history-anti-asian-discrimination -united-states.

[59] Ibid.

[60] Ibid.

[61] Rudolph, *Climate Change*.

[62] Ibid.

[63] "Japanese Internment Camps." *History*. Last modified on April 27, 2021. https://www.history.com/topics/world-war-ii/japanese -american-relocation.

[64] Ibid.

[65] Rudolph, *Climate Change*.

[66] Ibid.

[67] Ibid.

[68] Ibid.

[69] Watson, Ivan. "China: The Electronic Wastebasket of the World." *CNN*. Last modified on May 31, 2013. https://www.cnn .com/2013/05/30/world/asia/china-electronic-waste-e-waste /index.html.

[70] Ibid.

[71] Ibid.

[72] Ibid.

[73] "What's Causing Sea-Level Rise? Land Ice vs. Sea Ice." *Jet Propulsion Laboratory, California Institute of Technology*. Accessed May 21, 2021. https://www.jpl.nasa.gov/edu/teach/activity/whats-causing -sea-level-rise-land-ice-vs-sea-ice/#:~:text=Sea%20level%20 is%20rising%2C%20in,more%20water%20to%20Earth's%20 oceans.&text=As%20these%20ice%20sheets%20and,cause%20

sea%20level%20to%20rise.https://www.ncbi.nlm.nih.gov/pmc
/articles/PMC1280424/.

[74] Salem, Saber. "Climate Change and the Sinking Island States in the
Pacific." *E-International Relations*. Last modified on January 9,
2020. https://www.e-ir.info/2020/01/09/climate-change-and-the
-sinking-island-states-in-the-pacific/.

CHAPTER 5

[1] McFall-Johnsen, Morgan. "These Facts Show How Unsustainable the
Fashion Industry Is," World Economic Forum. Last modified on
January 31, 2020. https://www.weforum.org/agenda/2020/01
/fashion-industry-carbon-unsustainable-environment-pollution/.

[2] Hayes, Adam. "Fast Fashion." *Investopedia*. Last modified April 29,
2021. https://www.investopedia.com/terms/f/fast-fashion.asp.

[3] Ibid.

[4] Knutson, Brian; Scott Rick; G. Elliott Wimmer; Drazen Prelec; and
George Loewenstein. "Neural Predictors of Purchases." *Neuron*
no. 53.1 (2007): 147–156, doi: 10.1016/j.neuron.2006.11.010.

[5] Ibid.

[6] Bain, Marc, and *Quartz*. "The Neurological Pleasures of Fast Fashion."
The Atlantic. Last modified on March 25, 2015. https://www
.theatlantic.com/entertainment/archive/2015/03/the-neurologi
cal-pleasures-of-modern-shopping/388577/.

[7] Morgan, Andrew, director. 2015. *The True Cost*. Life Is My Movie Enter-
tainment.

[8] McFall-Johnsen, Morgan. "The Fashion Industry Emits More Carbon
than International Flights and Maritime Shipping Combined.
Here Are the Biggest Ways It Impacts the Planet." *Business Insider*. Last modified on October 21, 2019. https://www.business
insider.com/fast-fashion-environmental-impact-pollution-emis
sions-waste-water-2019-10.

[9] Ibid.

[10] "Fashion Industry, UN Pursue Climate Action for Sustainable Development." *United Nations Climate Change*. January 22, 2018.
https://unfccc.int/news/fashion-industry-un-pursue-climate
-action-for-sustainable-development.

[11] McFall-Johnsen, "The Fashion Industry."

[12] Linden, Annie Radner. "An Analysis of the Fast Fashion Industry." *Senior Projects Fall 2016*. 30. https://digitalcommons.bard.edu /senproj_f2016/30/.

[13] Reichart, Elizabeth, and Deborah Drew. "By the Numbers: The Economic, Social and Environmental Impacts of 'Fast Fashion.'" *World Resources Institute*. Last modified on January 10, 2019. https://www.wri.org/insights/numbers-economic-social-and -environmental-impacts-fast-fashion.

[14] Yardley, Jim. "Report on Deadly Factory Collapse in Bangladesh Finds Widespread Blame." *The New York Times*. Last modified on May 23, 2013. https://www.nytimes.com/2013/05/23/world/asia /report-on-bangladesh-building-collapse-finds-widespread -blame.html.

[15] "Violence in the Garment Industry: Infographic." *Global Fund for Women*. Accessed May 3, 2021. https://www.globalfundfor women.org/what-we-do/voice/campaigns/working-for-justice /garment-industry-violence-infographic/.

[16] George-Parkin, Hilary. "Size, by the Numbers." *Racked*. Last modified on June 5, 2018. https://www.racked.com/2018/6/5/17380662 /size-numbers-average-woman-plus-market.

[17] Chandran, Rina. "Indigenous People 'Under Threat' from Asia Clean Energy Push." Reuters. Last modified on February 9, 2021. https://www.reuters.com/article/us-landrights-renewables -environment-fea/indigenous-people-under-threat-from-asia -clean-energy-push-idUSKBN2A903H.

[18] Ibid.

[19] Tweedale, Aimee. "Biomass Energy: What Is It and How Does It Work?" *OVO Energy*. Last modified on November 26, 2020. https://www.ovoenergy.com/guides/energy-sources/bio-fuels .html.

[20] Chandran, "Indigenous People."

[21] English, Trevor. "Will Lithium Be the Next Oil?" *Interesting Engineering*. Last modified on January 11, 2020. https://interestingengi neering.com/will-lithium-be-the-next-oil.

[22] Palmer, Caroline. "Can Chile Avoid Resource Curse from Lithium?" *Reuters Events*. Last modified on March 16, 2021. https://www .reutersevents.com/sustainability/can-chile-avoid-resource-curse -lithium.

23 Katwala, Amit. "The Spiralling Environmental Cost of Our Lithium Battery Addiction." *Wired*. Last modified on August 5, 2018. https://www.wired.co.uk/article/lithium-batteries-environment-impact.

24 Palmer, "Can Chile Avoid Resource Curse?"

25 Horvath, Eniko, and Amanda Romero Medina. "Indigenous People's Livelihoods at Risk in Scramble for Lithium, the New White Gold." *Reuters Events*. Last modified on April 9, 2019. https://www.reutersevents.com/sustainability/indigenous-peoples-livelihoods-risk-scramble-lithium-new-white-gold.

26 Greenwood, Phoebe; Christopher Cherry; Maca Minguell; Charlie Phillips; Laurence Topham; and Tracy McVeigh. "Will Green Technology Kill Chile's Deserts?" *The Guardian*. February 18, 2020. Video, 11:55. https://www.theguardian.com/global-development/video/2020/feb/18/will-green-technology-kill-chiles-deserts-video?CMP=share_btn_tw&fbclid=IwAR31w7CPcLeolRm_kNmYc20LOZ45EKX-vBKmJFyciwUzS4gbUNS_3QXw5bI.

27 "Atacama, Chile." *Earthworks*. Accessed May 3, 2021. https://www.earthworks.org/stories/atacama-chile-lithium/.

28 Hitchcock Auciello, Benjamin. "Banks, Mining Executives, Car Companies, and the Rush to Mine Lithium in the Andean Salt Flats of Chile and Argentina." *Earthworks*. Last modified on February 27, 2020. https://www.earthworks.org/blog/banks-mining-executives-car-companies-and-the-rush-to-mine-lithium-in-the-andean-salt-flats-of-chile-and-argentina/.

29 Guzmán, Lorena. "Lithium Sparks Disputes in Chile's Atacama Desert." *Diálogo Chino*. Last modified on October 16, 2020. https://dialogochino.net/en/extractive-industries/37907-chiles-lithium-disputes/.

30 Sherwood, Dave. "Indigenous Groups in Chile's Atacama Push to Shut Down Top Lithium Miner SQM." Reuters. Last modified on August 14, 2020. https://www.reuters.com/article/us-chile-lithium-sqm/indigenous-groups-in-chiles-atacama-push-to-shut-down-top-lithium-miner-sqm-idUSKCN25A2PB.

31 Frankel, Todd C., and Peter Whoriskey. "Tossed Aside in the 'White Gold' Rush." *The Washington Post*. Last modified on December 19, 2016. https://www.washingtonpost.com/graphics/business/batteries/tossed-aside-in-the-lithium-rush/.

32 Gooderidge, Jack. "The Human Rights Abuses of Renewable Energy Companies in Mexico." *Mexico News Daily*. Last modified on

July 6, 2020. https://mexiconewsdaily.com/opinion/human
-rights-abuses-of-renewable-energy-companies/.

33 "Mareña Renovables in San Dionisio del Mar, Oaxaca, Mexico."
Environmental Justice Atlas. Last modified on March 29, 2017.
https://ejatlas.org/conflict/marena-renovables-in-san-dionisio
-del-mar-oaxaca.

34 "How Do Wind Turbines Work?" *Office of Energy Efficiency and Renewable Energy.* Accessed May 3, 2021. https://www.energy
.gov/eere/wind/how-do-wind-turbines-work.

35 "Rolando Crispín López." *HRD Memorial.* Accessed May 3, 2021.
https://hrdmemorial.org/hrdrecord/rolando-crispin-lopez/.

36 Ibid.

37 "Fifteen People Killed in Mexican Village Linked to Windpower Dis-
pute." *The Guardian.* Last modified on June 23, 2020. https://
www.theguardian.com/world/2020/jun/23/fifteen-people-killed
-in-mexican-village-linked-to-windpower-dispute.

38 Poore, Joseph, and Thomas Nemecek. "Reducing Food's Environmental Impacts Through Producers and Consumers." *Science* 360:
6392 (2018): 987–992, doi: 10.1126/science.aaq0216.

39 "Take Action in Your Home, School, or Community." *Climate Generation.* Accessed May 3, 2021. https://www.climategen.org
/take-action/act-climate-change/take-action/.

40 Petter, Olivia. "Veganism Is 'Single Biggest Way' to Reduce Our Environmental Impact, Study Finds." *The Independent.* Last modified on September 24, 2020. https://www.independent.co.uk
/life-style/health-and-families/veganism-environmental-impact
-planet-reduced-plant-based-diet-humans-study-a8378631
.html.

41 Arnet, Almuth, et al. *The IPCC Special Report on Climate Change, De-
sertification, Land Degradation, Sustainable Land Management,
Food Security, and Greenhouse Gas Fluxes in Terrestrial Ecosystems.* August 7, 2019. https://www.ipcc.ch/srccl-report-download
-page/.

42 Win, Thin Lei. "Fighting Global Warming, One Cow Belch at a Time."
Reuters. Last modified on July 19, 2018. https://www.reuters
.com/article/us-global-livestock-emissions/fighting-global-warm
ing-one-cow-belch-at-a-time-idUSKBN1K91CU.

43 Oberst, Lindsay. "Why the Global Rise in Vegan and Plant-Based
Eating Isn't a Fad (600% Increase in U.S. Vegans + Other

Astounding Stats)." *Food Revolution Network*. Last modified on January 18, 2018. https://foodrevolution.org/blog/vegan-statistics-global/.

[44] Ibid.

[45] McCarthy, Justin, and Scott Dekoster. "Nearly One in Four in U.S. Have Cut Back on Eating Meat." Gallup. Last modified on January 27, 2020. https://news.gallup.com/poll/282779/nearly-one-four-cut-back-eating-meat.aspx.

[46] "Why Black Americans Are More Likely to Be Vegan." *BBC*. September 11, 2020. https://www.bbc.com/news/world-us-canada-53787329.

[47] Ibid.

[48] Richter, Felix. "Where Vegetarianism Is Booming." *Statista*. Last modified on October 1, 2019. https://www.statista.com/chart/18852/countries-with-the-biggest-increase-of-the-vegetarian-population-between-2016-and-2017/.

[49] "Which Countries Have the Most Vegetarians?" *Radio Free Europe /Radio Liberty*. January 21, 2019. https://www.rferl.org/a/which-countries-have-the-most-vegetarians/29722181.html.

[50] "History." *The Vegan Society*. Accessed May 3, 2021. https://www.vegansociety.com/about-us/history.

[51] Nowakowski, Kelsey. "For Rastas, Eating Pure Food from the Earth Is a Sacred Duty." *National Geographic*. Last modified on July 19, 2016. https://www.nationalgeographic.com/culture/article/for-rastas--eating-from-the-earth-is-a-sacred-duty.

[52] Mitchell, Charlie. "Is the Vegan Movement Ready to Reckon with Racism?" Civil Eats. Last modified on August 26, 2020. https://civileats.com/2020/08/26/is-the-vegan-movement-ready-to-reckon-with-racism/.

ABOUT THE AUTHOR

LEAH THOMAS is an intersectional environmental educator, writer, and creative based in Southern California. She's passionate about advocating for and exploring the relationship between social justice and environmentalism and was the first to define the term "intersectional environmentalism." She is the founder of @greengirlleah and the Intersectional Environmentalist platform. Her articles on this topic have appeared in *Vogue, Elle, The Good Trade, Marie Claire,* and *Highsnobiety,* and she has been featured by *Harper's Bazaar, W* magazine, *Domino, Goop, Fashionista,* CNN, *BuzzFeed,* and numerous podcasts. She has a BS in environmental science and policy from Chapman University and worked for the National Park Service and Patagonia headquarters before pursuing environmental education full-time.